G000055687

STEP-BY-STEP
50 Classic Cakes

STEP-BY-STEP
50 Classic Cakes

Consultant Editor
Linda Fraser

HERMES
HOUSE

This edition published by Hermes House
an imprint of
Anness Publishing Limited
Hermes House
88-89 Blackfriars Road
London SE1 8HA

All rights reserved. No part of this publication may be reproduced,
stored in a retrieval system, or transmitted in any way or by any means,
electronic, mechanical, photocopying, recording or otherwise, without
the prior written permission of the copyright holder.

A CIP catalogue record for this book is available from the British Library

ISBN 1-901289-64-8

Publisher: Joanna Lorenz
Senior Cookery Editor: Linda Fraser
In-house Editor: Margaret Malone
Designer: Brian Weldon
Recipes: Carla Capalbo, Jacqueline Clark, Carol Clements, Joanna Farrow,
Shirley Gill, Carole Handslip, Patricia Lousada, Norma MacMillan,
Sarah Maxwell, Janice Murfitt, Angela Nilsen, Louise Pickford,
Hilaire Walden, Laura Washburn, Judy Williams and Elizabeth Wolf-Cohen
Photographers: Karl Adamson, Edward Allwright, David Armstrong,
Steve Baxter, Michelle Garrett, Amanda Heywood and Tim Hill

Printed in Hong Kong / China

© Anness Publishing Limited 1997
Updated © 1999
3 5 7 9 10 8 6 4

For all recipes, quantities are in both metric and imperial measures, and,
where appropriate, measures, are also given in standard cups and spoons.
Follow one set, but not a mixture, because they are not interchangeable.

CONTENTS

INTRODUCTION

A home-made cake is an irresistible but, sadly, an all too rare treat. Our busy lifestyles, our attempts at healthy eating and calorie counting and sometimes a lack of confidence when it comes to baking, have all helped to convince us that a home-made cake is a thing of the past. This book, however, shows that with a little knowledge of basic cake-making skills, delicious classic cakes can be created easily. Not only will you have fun making the cake, but you will be amazed at how enthusiastically it is received.

One common misconception is that making a cake is difficult, but this needn't be the case. Most of the cakes that we all know and love are based on simple time-honoured cake and icing recipes such as Quick-mix and Whisked Sponge cake, Madeira cake, Swiss roll and Fruit cake and icings such as Butter and Glacé icing. *Step-by-step 50 Classic Cakes* introduces the home cook to these essential cake and icing recipes, with easy to follow step-by-step instructions. The helpful introduction sets out some basic guidelines, including information on ingredients, equipment, testing and storing cakes. These guidelines are very simple to follow, and from there it is a short step to creating such delicious classic treats as Angel Cake, Sachertorte and Mocha-hazelnut Battenburg.

Learn a few of the simple icing techniques contained in this book, and see how easy it is to transform a cake. Be it drizzling lemon glacé over a traditional gingerbread loaf or generously coating a cake with chocolate fudge icing topped with chocolate curls, you will be amazed at the effects you can create.

Cake-making should be fun and enjoyable. *Step-by-step 50 Classic Cakes* explains all the basic skills necessary for baking delicious cakes plus fifty tempting recipes to choose from. So, turn the pages, and bring a smile of delight to the faces of friends and family around you.

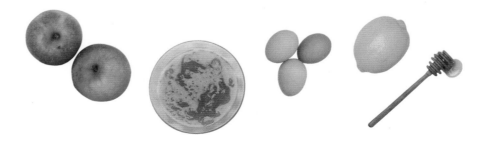

Store Cupboard

Many of the most useful and important baking ingredients are found in the store cupboard. The following guide highlights a few of the most essential items.

cracked wheat   *olives*   *flour*

bottled apricots

dried pineapple   *dried yeast*

FLOURS

Mass-produced, highly refined flours are fine for most baking purposes, but for the very best results choose organic stone-ground flours because they will add flavour as well as texture to your baking.

Strong flour

Made from hard wheat, which contains a high proportion of gluten, this flour is the one to use for bread-making.

Soft flour

This flour, sometimes called sponge flour, contains less gluten than plain flour and is ideal for light cakes and biscuits.

Wholemeal flour

Because this flour contains the complete wheat kernel, it gives a coarser texture and a good wholesome flavour to bread.

Rye flour

This dark-coloured flour has a low gluten content and gives a dense loaf with a good flavour. It is best mixed with strong wheat flour to give a lighter loaf.

NUTS

Most nuts are low in saturated fats and high in polyunsaturated fats. Use them sparingly as their total fat content is high.

HERBS AND SPICES

Chopped fresh herbs add a great deal of interest to baking. They add flavour to breads, scones and soda breads. In the absence of fresh herbs, dried herbs can be used: less is needed but the flavour is generally not as good.

Spices can add either strong or subtle flavours depending on the amount and variety used. Ground cinnamon, nutmeg and mixed spice are most useful for baking, but more exotic spices, such as saffron or cardamom, can also be used to great effect.

SWEETENERS

Unrefined sugars

Most baking recipes call for sugar; choose unrefined sugar, rather than refined sugars, as they have more flavour and contain some minerals.

Honey

Good honey has a strong flavour so you can use rather less of it than the equivalent amount of sugar. It also contains traces of minerals and vitamins.

Malt extract

This is a sugary by-product of barley. It has a strong flavour and is good to use in bread, cakes and teabreads as it adds a moistness of its own.

Molasses

This is the residue left after the first stage of refining sugar cane. It has a strong, smoky and slightly bitter taste which gives a good flavour to bakes and cakes. Black treacle can often be used as a substitute for molasses.

Fruit juice

Concentrated fruit juices are very useful for baking. They have no added sweeteners or preservatives and can be diluted as required. Use them in their concentrated form for baking or for sweetening fillings.

Pear and apple spread

This is a very concentrated fruit juice with no added sugar. It has a sweet-sour taste and can be used as a spread or blended with a little fruit juice and added to baking recipes as a sweetener.

Dried fruits

These are a traditional addition to cakes and teabreads and there is a very wide range available, including some more unusual varieties such as peach, pineapple, banana, mango and pawpaw. The natural sugars add sweetness to baked goods and keep them moist, making it possible to use less fat.

eggs

light muscovado

currants

poppy seeds

honey

herbs

fresh fruit

oatmeal

cinnamon sticks

dried apricots

sesame seeds

chestnuts

sunflower

linseed

raisins

glacé cherries

olive oil

pear and apple spread

apricot compôte

dates

garlic

extra
virgin
olive oil

fresh fruit

red
onions

rolled oats

orange juice

blueberries

semolina

Equipment

Baking sheet
Choose a large, heavy baking sheet that will not warp at high temperatures.

Balloon whisk
Perfect for whisking egg whites and incorporating air into other light mixtures.

Box grater
This multi-purpose grater can be used for citrus rind, fruit and vegetables, and cheese.

Brown paper
Used for wrapping around the outside of cake tins to protect the cake mixture from the full heat of the oven.

Cake tester
A simple implement which, when inserted into a cooked cake, will come out clean if the cake is ready.

Cook's knife
This has a heavy, wide blade and is ideal for chopping.

Deep round cake tin
This type of tin is ideal for baking fruit cakes.

Electric whisk
Ideal for creaming cake mixtures, whipping cream and whisking egg whites.

Honey twirl
For spooning honey without making a mess!

Juicer
Made from porcelain, glass or plastic and used for squeezing the juice from citrus fruits.

Loaf tin
Available in various sizes and used for making loaf-shaped breads and teabreads.

Measuring jug
Essential for measuring any kind of liquid accurately.

Measuring spoons
Standard measuring spoons are essential for measuring small quantities of ingredients.

Metal spoons
Large metal spoons are perfect for folding as they minimize the amount of air that escapes.

Mixing bowls
A set of different sized bowls is essential in any kitchen for whisking, mixing and so on.

Muffin tin
Shaped into individual cups, this tin is much simpler to use than individual paper cases. It can also be used for baking small pies and tarts.

Non-stick baking paper
For lining tins and baking sheets to ensure cakes, meringues and biscuits do not stick.

Nutmeg grater
This miniature grater is used for grating whole nutmegs.

Nylon sieve
Suitable for most baking purposes, and particularly for sieving foods which react adversely with metal.

Palette knife
This implement is needed for loosening pies, tarts and breads from baking sheets and for smoothing icing over cakes.

Pastry brush
Useful for brushing excess flour from pastry and brushing glazes over pastries, breads and tarts.

Pastry cutters
A variety of shapes and sizes of cutter are useful when stamping out pastry, biscuits and scones.

Rectangular cake tin
For making tray bakes and cakes, served cut into slices.

Ring mould
Perfect for making angel cakes and other ring-shaped cakes.

Sandwich cake tin
Ideal for sponge cakes; make sure you have two of them!

Scissors
Vital for cutting paper and snipping doughs and pastry.

Square cake tin
Used for making square cakes or cakes served cut into squares.

Swiss roll tin
This shallow tin is designed especially for Swiss rolls.

Vegetable knife
A useful knife for preparing the fruit and vegetables which you may add to your bakes.

Wire rack
Ideal for cooling cakes and bakes, allowing circulation of air to prevent sogginess.

Wire sieve
A large wire sieve is ideal for most baking purposes.

Wooden spoon
Essential for mixing ingredients and creaming mixtures.

rectangular cake tin

square cake tin

loaf tin

baking sheet

balloon whisk

large metal spoon   *wooden spoon*

electric whisk

mixing bowls

non-stick baking paper

brown paper

scissors

sandwich cake tin

pastry brush

ring mould

measuring jug

wire rack

deep round cake tin

cake tester

pastry cutters

vegetable knife

honey twirl

wire rack

Swiss roll tin

juicer

wire sieve

nutmeg grater

cook's knife

palette knives

box grater

nylon sieve

measuring spoons

muffin tin

Successful Baking

There are a few simple guidelines which must be followed to achieve the best results when making any cake.

Before You Start

- Always make sure you have the correct shape and size of tin for the recipe as this will affect the depth of the cake, the cooking time and the texture.

- Make sure the tin is properly prepared and lined for cooking your chosen recipe.

- Check that you have all the necessary ingredients listed in the recipe, and that they are at the right temperature.

- Eggs should be size 3, unless otherwise stated. Farm eggs impart a wonderful flavour, but unless they are graded they may be too large for cakes, making the mixture slack.

- Do check that your oven is at the correct temperature before cooking the cake. If your oven is fan-assisted, you may need to reduce the temperature; check your handbook.

Mixing Cakes Successfully

- Unlike many recipes, those for cakes must be followed accurately. Measure all the ingredients carefully with scales or measuring cups, spoons and a measuring jug.

- Ensure that soft margarine is kept chilled in the fridge to maintain the right consistency, and leave butter out so that it reaches room temperature and becomes soft for creaming.

- When making cakes by hand, beat well with a wooden spoon until the mixture is light and glossy; scrape down the mixture during beating with a plastic spatula to ensure even mixing.

- If a cake is being made in a food processor or an electric mixer, be very careful not to overprocess or overbeat. This will cause the mixture to collapse and dip in the middle during baking. Remember to scrape down the batter with a plastic spatula during mixing.

- Sift all dry ingredients to help aerate the mixture and to disperse lumps. Tapping the sieve will speed up the process.

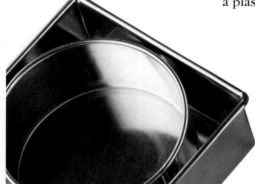

- If ingredients have to be folded into a mixture, use a metal spoon or plastic spatula with a flexible blade to cut through the mixture, turning it over and at the same time moving the bowl. Do not be tempted to stir or be heavy-handed with the mixture or it will lose air and become heavy.

- Level mixtures in the tin before baking, to ensure the cake rises evenly. With some fruit cake mixtures, you will be advised to make a small hollow in the centre of the cake; this will fill in as it bakes to give a level surface.

Checking your Oven

Many of the problems which may arise when cooking cakes do so because ovens vary. Factors affecting cooking results include the heat source. Some ovens are hot, others are slow, others are fan-assisted. Recipes always give cooking times, but you must remember that these are simply a guide. The guidelines below assume the recipes and tin sizes have been followed as advised.

- Do check that your oven is preheated to the temperature stated in the recipe. Failure to do so will affect the rising of the cake and the cooking time.

- If the cake appears to be cooked before the given time, it may indicate that the oven is too hot; conversely, if the cake takes longer to cook, it means the oven is slow.

- A good test is to cook a home-made two-egg quick-mix cake in a 20 cm/8 in sandwich tin for about 35–40 minutes at 160°C/325°F/Gas 3. The cake should appear level and lightly browned. If the cake is cooked before the time, adjust the setting lower in the future, or higher for a cake which takes longer. If using a fan-assisted oven, consult your handbook.

- The temperature of the cake mixture can cause the cooking time to vary. If conditions are cold, the mixture will be cold and take longer to cook; in the same way, if it is warm, cooking time will be slightly quicker.

- Test the cake before the stated cooking time and before removing it from the oven. Test as advised in the recipe, by appearance, touch, or inserting a skewer, which should come out clean.

✔ Ten point checklist

- ☐ Follow recipe instructions accurately
- ☐ Ensure that you have all the right ingredients and equipment; set them out in order of use
- ☐ Check that ingredients are at the right temperature
- ☐ Be careful not to overprocess or overbeat when using a food processor or electric mixer
- ☐ When folding, incorporate as much air as possible into the mixture

- ☐ Make sure you have the correct shape and size of tin for the recipe
- ☐ Level the mixture in the tin before baking
- ☐ Make sure your oven is preheated to the correct temperature
- ☐ Where possible, bake in the centre of the oven where the heat is more likely to be constant
- ☐ Test the cake before the stated cooking time and immediately before removing from the oven

Lining Cake Tins

Cake tins are lined in different ways, depending on the type of cake you are making. Sometimes tins are only lightly greased and floured, as when making a light whisked sponge cake mixture. In this way the shape holds to the sides of the tin during cooking: if paper lined, it would pull away, producing a misshapen cake.

Most cakes, however, are baked in tins lined with greaseproof or non-stick baking paper. Sometimes only the base is covered for a cake requiring short-term cooking. Both the base and sides are lined when cakes need longer cooking, or for richer cake mixtures which may stick to the tin. Swiss roll tins have to be lined neatly with one piece of paper so the cake can be turned out of the tin quickly to form into a roll. Cakes which need long-term cooking, such as fruit cakes, require a double thickness of paper inside the tin and the protection of double thickness brown paper around the outside of the tin so that the cake cooks evenly throughout.

Generally, cake tins are brushed with melted vegetable fat or oil before they are lined with greaseproof or non-stick baking paper.

Lining a Sandwich Tin

1 Place the tin on a piece of greaseproof or non-stick baking paper. Using a pencil, draw around the base of the tin. Cut out the circle using a pair of sharp scissors.

2 Brush the tin lightly with melted vegetable fat or oil and fit the paper circle in the bottom of the tin. Grease the paper lightly.

Lining a Swiss Roll Tin

1 Place the tin in the centre of a piece of greaseproof or non-stick baking paper, 2.5 cm/1 in larger all round than the tin. Cut from the corner of the paper to the corner of the tin, using a pair of sharp scissors.

2 Lightly brush the tin with melted vegetable fat or oil and fit the paper into the tin, neatly pressing it into the corners. Grease the paper lightly.

Lining a Deep Round or Square Cake Tin

1 Cut two paper circles or squares for the bottom of the tin (see below), then cut a strip, a little longer than the tin's circumference and one-and-a-half times its depth. Make small diagonal cuts along the edge of the paper strip.

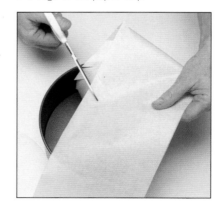

2 Lightly grease the tin and place one paper shape on the bottom. Fit the paper strip inside the tin, with the snipped fringe flat along the bottom. Place the second paper shape on top, to cover the fringe. Grease once more.

Cook's Tip

If the cake has a long cooking time, protect it by placing a strip of double thickness brown paper around the tin, keeping it in place with string.

Testing Cakes

It is very important to check that cakes and bakes are properly cooked, otherwise they can be soggy and may sink in the middle.

Testing a Fruit Cake

1 To test if a fruit cake is ready, push a skewer or cake tester into it; if it comes out clean, the cake is cooked.

2 Fruit cakes are generally left to cool in the tin for 30 minutes. Then turn the cake out carefully, peel away the paper and place on a wire rack or board.

Testing a Sponge Cake

1 To test if a sponge cake is ready, press down lightly on the centre of the cake with your fingertips – if the cake springs back, it is cooked.

2 To remove the cooked sponge cake from the tin, loosen around the edge by carefully running round the inside of the tin with a palette knife. Invert the cake on to a wire rack, cover with a second rack, then invert again. Remove the top rack and leave to cool.

Storing Cakes

Everyday cakes, sponges and meringues can be kept in an airtight container or simply wrapped in cling film or foil: the exclusion of air will ensure that they keep moist and fresh. Store the cakes in a cool, dry place for up to a week; meringues will store for up to one month. Avoid warm, moist conditions as this will encourage mould to grow.

- To store fruit cakes, leave the lining paper on the cakes. Wrap the cakes in a double layer of foil and keep in a cool place. Never seal a fruit cake in an airtight container for long periods of time as this may encourage mould growth.

- Rich, heavy fruit cakes can be happily stored for up to three months. If you are going to keep a fruit cake for several months before marzipanning or icing it, pour over alcohol, such as brandy, a little at a time at monthly intervals, turning the cake each time.

- Light fruit cakes are at their best when first made, or eaten within one month of making.

- For long-term storage, fruit cakes are better frozen in their double wrapping and foil.

- Once the cakes have been marzipanned and iced, they will keep longer, but iced cakes must be stored in cardboard cake boxes in a warm, dry atmosphere. Damp and cold are the worst conditions, causing the icing to stain and colourings to run.

- Freeze a decorated celebration cake in the cake box, ensuring the lid is sealed with tape. Take the cake out of its box and thaw it slowly in a cool, dry place. When the cake has thawed, transfer it to a warm, dry place so that the icing dries completely.

Quick Icing Techniques

Icing is easy if you start with simple decorations and build up to more elaborate work as your confidence grows.

● Use a metal palette knife to spread icing over a cake. Keep the icing even and smooth.

● Spoon whipped cream along the centre of a Swiss roll and dot with fresh raspberries for a delightful decoration that takes only minutes.

● Place strips of greaseproof paper over the top of a sponge cake at equal distances and dust liberally with icing sugar. Carefully lift off the strips of paper, without smudging the icing sugar.

● Use chopped walnuts to clever effect: cover the sides of a sponge cake with coffee icing and roll the sides of the cake over the chopped nuts to coat.

Using Chocolate to Decorate Cakes

Chocolate is a versatile ingredient to work with. It is sold in many forms – milk, plain and white; in bars, chips, as thick, richly flavoured spreads, and as powdered cocoa and drinking chocolate.

To Melt Chocolate

● Break the chocolate into very small pieces and place in a heatproof bowl over a saucepan of hand-hot water. Ensure that the base of the bowl does not touch the water. Stir occasionally until the chocolate has all melted.
● Chocolate can be melted in a microwave set at the lowest setting if time is short, but only if the chocolate is being used to add to other ingredients. For coating and spreading, the chocolate becomes too warm and when the surface dries it looks streaky.

Dipping Fruit

● Have everything ready before starting. All items to be dipped should be at room temperature, otherwise the chocolate will set before smoothly coating. Use a confectioner's dipping fork or a large dinner fork and have several sheets of non-stick baking paper ready to take the dipped items.

● Dip items, such as strawberries, individually into melted chocolate; turn once with the dipping fork to coat evenly. Lift out on the fork and tap gently on the side of the bowl to allow the excess chocolate to fall. Place on the paper and leave to set.

Chocolate Curls

● When the chocolate has just set, but has not become hard, hold a sharp cook's knife at a 45° angle to the chocolate. Draw the knife across the surface to shave off thin curls.
● Pour melted chocolate on to a rigid surface such as marble, wood or plastic laminate. Spread evenly backwards and forwards with a palette knife until smooth.
● To make chocolate shavings, let the chocolate set a little harder before beginning. Then draw the knife only halfway across the surface to shave off fine chocolate flakes.

Making an Icing Bag

Being able to make your own piping bag is a very handy skill, particularly if you are dealing with small amounts of icing or several colours.

Creating Special Effects

Confident icing of a cake makes all the difference to its appearance. With just a little practice, your cakes will look completely professional!

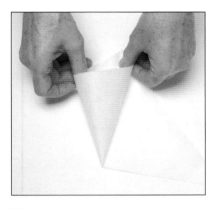

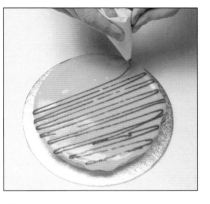

1 Fold a 25 cm/10 in square of grease-proof paper in half to form a triangle. Using the centre of the long side as the central tip, roll half the paper into a cone.

2 Holding the paper in position, continue to roll the other half of the triangle around the first half to complete the cone neatly.

1 To create a simple zig-zag effect, ice the cake all over, then pipe lines in a different colour backwards and forwards over the top.

2 To create a feathered effect, follow step 1, then drag a knife through the icing at regular intervals in opposite directions, perpendicular to the lines.

3 To make a figure of eight, or a similar effect, ice the cake all over then, using a different coloured icing, pipe figures of eight around the edge of the cake, in a steady stream.

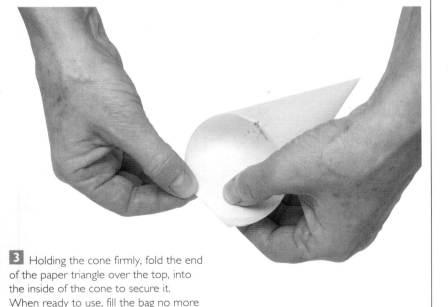

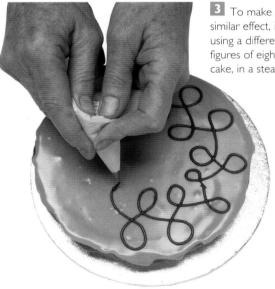

3 Holding the cone firmly, fold the end of the paper triangle over the top, into the inside of the cone to secure it. When ready to use, fill the bag no more than half full with icing, fold over the top several times to seal, then snip off the tip of the bag to the required size.

BASIC CAKE RECIPES

QUICK-MIX SPONGE CAKE

This is a quick and easy, reliable recipe for making everyday cakes in various sizes, shapes and flavours. The quantity can be increased if necessary, provided the proportions remain the same.

Makes one 15 cm/6 in square or 18 cm/7 in round cake

INGREDIENTS

175 g/6 oz/1½ cups self-raising flour
7.5 ml/1½ tsp baking powder
175 g/6 oz/¾ cup caster sugar
175 g/6 oz/¾ cup soft margarine
3 eggs

1 Preheat the oven to 160°C/325°F/ Gas 3. Prepare the tin according to the recipe. Sift the flour and baking powder into a bowl. Add the sugar, margarine and eggs. Mix with a wooden spoon, then beat for 1–2 minutes until smooth and glossy.

2 Stir in your chosen flavouring and beat until evenly blended. Pour the mixture into the prepared tin, level the top and bake as required.

FLAVOURINGS
Citrus Add 10 ml/2 tsp finely grated orange, lemon or lime rind.
Coffee Add 10 ml/2 tsp instant coffee granules blended with 5 ml/1 tsp boiling water.
Chocolate Add 15 ml/1 tbsp cocoa powder blended with 15 ml/1 tbsp boiling water, or 25 g/1 oz/scant ¼ cup chocolate chips, melted.

WHISKED SPONGE CAKE

This light sponge is the classic base for making Swiss rolls but can also be used for cakes or gâteaux.

Makes one 33 x 23 cm/13 x 9 in Swiss roll cake

INGREDIENTS
3 eggs
75 g/3 oz/⅓ cup caster sugar
75 g/3 oz/¾ cup plain flour

1 Preheat the oven to 180°C/350°F/ Gas 4. Prepare the tin according to the recipe. Whisk the eggs and sugar in a heatproof bowl. Place the bowl over a saucepan of simmering water and whisk until thick and pale. Remove the bowl from the saucepan and continue whisking until the mixture is cool and leaves a thick trail on the surface when the beaters are lifted.

2 Sift the flour over the surface, add any desired flavouring, then carefully fold the flour into the mixture until smooth.

3 Pour into the chosen tin, tilt to level the mixture and bake as required.

COOK'S TIP
Like the Quick-mix Sponge Cake, the Whisked Sponge can be adapted for a smaller or larger tin by altering the quantities. Just remember to keep the ratio of 1 egg to each 25 g/ 1 oz of sugar and flour.

MADEIRA CAKE

This is a good, plain cake which can be made as an alternative to a light or rich fruit cake. Firm and moist, it makes an excellent base for icing and decorating.

Makes one 15 cm/6 in square or 18 cm/7 in round cake

INGREDIENTS
225 g/8 oz/2 cups plain flour
5 ml/1 tsp baking powder
175 g/6 oz/¾ cup caster sugar
175 g/6 oz/¾ cup soft margarine
3 eggs
30 ml/2 tbsp milk

1 Preheat the oven to 160°C/325°F/ Gas 3. Grease and line a deep cake tin. Sift the flour and baking powder into a mixing bowl. Add the sugar, margarine, eggs and milk. Mix with a wooden spoon, then beat for 1–2 minutes until smooth and glossy. Alternatively, use an electric mixer and beat for 1 minute only.

2 Add any desired flavouring and mix well. Place the mixture into the prepared tin and spread evenly. Give the tin a sharp tap to remove any air pockets. Bake the cake for 1¼–1½ hours or until the cake springs back when lightly pressed in the centre.

FLAVOURINGS

Cherry Add 175 g/6 oz/scant 1 cup glacé cherries, halved.
Citrus Replace the milk with lemon, orange or lime juice and add 5 ml/1 tsp grated lemon, orange or lime rind.
Coconut Add 50 g/2 oz/⅔ cup desiccated coconut.

RICH FRUIT CAKE

This recipe makes a very moist, rich cake suitable for any celebration.

Makes one 18 cm/7 in square or 20 cm/8 in round cake

INGREDIENTS
200 g/7 oz/1 cup each raisins,
    sultanas and currants
115 g/4 oz/½ cup glacé cherries
50 g/2 oz/½ cup cut mixed peel
50 g/2 oz/⅔ cup flaked almonds
grated rind and juice of 1 lemon
45 ml/3 tbsp brandy or sherry
200 g/7 oz/1¾ cups plain flour
5 ml/1 tsp ground mixed spice
50 g/2 oz/⅔ cup ground almonds
175 g/6 oz/scant 1 cup light brown
    sugar
200 g/7 oz/scant 1 cup butter
30 ml/2 tbsp black treacle
4 eggs

2 Preheat the oven to 140°C/275°F/ Gas 1. Prepare a deep cake tin. Sift the flour and mixed spice into a mixing bowl. Add the ground almonds, sugar, butter, treacle and eggs. Mix well, then beat for 1–2 minutes. Add the fruit mixture and mix again.

1 Mix the dried fruit, glacé cherries, mixed peel, flaked almonds, lemon rind and juice in a bowl. Stir in the brandy or sherry. Cover and leave to stand for several hours or overnight.

3 Spoon the mixture into the tin and make a slight depression in the centre. Bake for 4–4½ hours or until a skewer inserted in the centre comes out clean. Cover the surface lightly with foil if it starts to over-brown.

BASIC ICINGS

BUTTER ICING

This most popular and well-known icing is made quickly with butter and icing sugar. Add your choice of flavourings and colourings to vary the cake.

Makes 450 g/1 lb

INGREDIENTS
115 g/4 oz/½ cup butter, softened
225 g/8 oz/2 cups icing sugar, sifted
10 ml/2 tsp milk
5 ml/1 tsp vanilla essence

AMERICAN FROSTING

This light marshmallow mixture crisps on the outside when left to dry. The frosting can be swirled or peaked into a soft coating.

Makes 350 g/12 oz

INGREDIENTS
1 egg white
30 ml/2 tbsp water
15 ml/1 tbsp golden syrup
5 ml/1 tsp cream of tartar
175 g/6 oz/1½ cups icing sugar

1 Place the butter in a bowl. Using a wooden spoon or an electric mixer, beat until light and fluffy.

2 Stir in the icing sugar, milk and vanilla essence, with any flavouring. Mix, then beat well until light and smooth. Spread the icing over the cake.

1 Place the egg white, water, golden syrup and cream of tartar in a heatproof bowl. Whisk together until thoroughly blended. Stir in the icing sugar and place the bowl over a saucepan of simmering water. Whisk until the mixture becomes thick and white.

2 Turn off the heat and continue to whisk the frosting for 2 minutes, then remove the bowl from the pan and whisk until the frosting is cool and thick, and stands up in soft peaks. Use immediately.

FLAVOURINGS

Citrus Replace the milk and vanilla essence with orange, lemon or lime juice. Add 10 ml/ 2 tsp finely grated orange, lemon or lime rind. Omit the rind if the icing is to be piped.
Chocolate Add 15 ml/1 tbsp cocoa powder blended with 15 ml/1 tbsp boiling water, and cooled.
Coffee Add 10 ml/2 tsp coffee granules blended with 15 ml/ 1 tbsp boiling water, and cooled.

GLACÉ ICING

An instant icing for quickly finishing the tops of large or small cakes, this is also used to make feathered icing by introducing a second, coloured, icing to obtain the feathered effect.

Makes 350 g/12 oz

INGREDIENTS
225 g/8 oz/2 cups icing sugar
30–45 ml/2–3 tbsp hot water
food colouring (optional)

1 Sift the icing sugar into a bowl. Using a wooden spoon, gradually stir in enough hot water to obtain the consistency of thick cream. It is easy to add too much liquid, so be careful.

2 Beat until the icing is smooth and thickly coats the back of a wooden spoon. Colour with a few drops of food colouring if desired. Use immediately to cover the top of the cake.

CHOCOLATE FUDGE ICING

A rich, glossy icing which sets like chocolate fudge, this is versatile enough to coat smoothly, swirl or pipe, depending on the temperature of the icing when it is used.

Makes 450 g/1 lb

INGREDIENTS
115 g/4 oz plain chocolate
50 g/2 oz/4 tbsp butter
1 egg, beaten
175 g/6 oz/1½ cups icing sugar,
    sifted

1 Place the chocolate and butter in a heatproof bowl over a saucepan of hot water. Stir occasionally with a wooden spoon until melted. Add the egg and beat until smooth.

2 Remove the bowl from the saucepan and stir in the icing sugar, then beat until smooth and glossy. Pour immediately over the cake for a smooth finish, or leave to cool for a thicker spreading or piping consistency.

COOK'S TIP
Raw or lightly cooked eggs can pose a health risk which pregnant women, the elderly and very young may prefer to avoid.

Pear and Sultana Teabread

This is an ideal teabread to make when pears are plentiful – an excellent use for windfalls.

Serves 6–8

INGREDIENTS
25 g/1 oz/scant ⅓ cup rolled oats
50 g/2 oz/⅓ cup light muscovado
 sugar
30 ml/2 tbsp pear or apple juice
30 ml/2 tbsp sunflower oil
1 large or 2 small pears
115 g/4 oz/1 cup self-raising flour
115 g/4 oz/⅔ cup sultanas
2.5 ml/½ tsp baking powder
10 ml/2 tsp ground mixed spice
1 egg

egg

baking powder

pears

sunflower oil

self-raising flour

rolled oats

sultanas

ground mixed spice

pear juice

light muscovado sugar

1 Preheat the oven to 180°C/350°F/Gas 4. Grease and line a 450 g/1 lb loaf tin with non-stick baking paper. Put the oats in a bowl with the sugar, pour over the pear or apple juice and oil, mix well and leave to stand for 15 minutes until some of the liquid is absorbed.

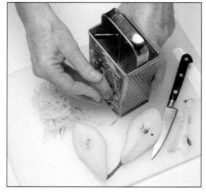

2 Quarter, core and grate the pear(s). Add to the oat mixture with the flour, sultanas, baking powder, mixed spice and egg, then mix together thoroughly.

3 Spoon the mixture into the prepared loaf tin and level the top. Bake for 50–60 minutes or until a skewer inserted into the centre comes out clean.

4 Transfer the teabread on to a wire rack and peel off the lining paper. Leave to cool completely.

COOK'S TIP

Health food shops sell concentrated pear and apple juice, ready for diluting as required.

Banana and Ginger Teabread

Serve this teabread in slices with butter. The stem ginger adds an interesting flavour.

Serves 6–8

INGREDIENTS
175 g/6 oz/1½ cups self-raising flour
5 ml/1 tsp baking powder
40 g/1½ oz/3 tbsp soft margarine
50 g/2 oz/⅓ cup dark muscovado
   sugar
50 g/2 oz/⅓ cup drained stem
   ginger, chopped
60 ml/4 tbsp milk
2 ripe bananas, mashed

baking powder

stem ginger

dark muscovado sugar

bananas

self-raising flour

milk

soft margarine

COOK'S TIP

To make Banana and Sultana Teabread, add 5 ml/1 tsp ground mixed spice and 115 g/4 oz/⅔ cup sultanas; omit the stem ginger.

1 Preheat the oven to 180°C/350°F/ Gas 4. Grease and line a 450 g/1 lb loaf tin. Sift the flour and baking powder into a mixing bowl.

2 Rub in the margarine until the mixture resembles breadcrumbs.

3 Stir in the sugar. Add the ginger, milk and bananas and mix to a soft dough.

4 Spoon into the prepared tin and bake for 40–45 minutes. Run a palette knife around the edges to loosen then turn the teabread on to a wire rack and leave to cool.

Madeira Cake

In the nineteenth century, this cake was served mid-morning with a glass of Madeira wine.

Serves 6

INGREDIENTS
175 g/6 oz/¾ cup butter
175 g/6 oz/¾ cup caster sugar
4 eggs, beaten
grated rind of 1 lemon
225 g/8 oz/2 cups self-raising flour
pinch of salt
2 strips candied peel

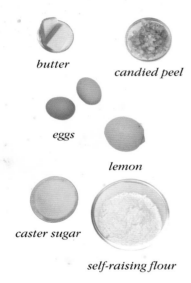

butter

candied peel

eggs

lemon

caster sugar

self-raising flour

1 Preheat the oven to 180°C/350°F/Gas 4. Grease and line an 18 cm/7 in round cake tin. Beat the butter and sugar until light and fluffy, then gradually beat in the eggs, adding the lemon rind and a little of the flour towards the end. Fold in the remaining flour and the salt, then turn into the prepared cake tin and smooth the surface.

2 Bake the cake for 30 minutes, until set, then carefully place the peel on the top. Bake for a further 10 minutes, then reduce the oven temperature to 160°C/325°F/Gas 3 and continue to bake until firm in the centre.

3 Leave the cake to cool slightly in the tin, then turn on to a wire rack and carefully remove the lining paper.

COOK'S TIP
Madeira cake is famous for its keeping properties. Store it in an airtight tin. Some cooks swear that adding an apple to the tin keeps the cake from getting too dry.

Lemon Meringue Cakes

This is a variation on fairy cakes – soft lemon sponge topped with crisp meringue.

Makes 18

INGREDIENTS
115 g/4 oz/½ cup margarine
200 g/7 oz/scant 1 cup caster sugar
2 eggs, plus 2 egg whites
115 g/4 oz/1 cup self-raising flour
5 ml/1 tsp baking powder
grated rind of 2 lemons
30 ml/2 tbsp lemon juice

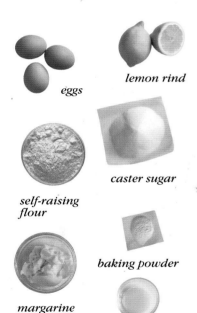

eggs

lemon rind

caster sugar

self-raising
flour

baking powder

margarine

lemon juice

1 Preheat the oven to 190°C/375°F/ Gas 5. Put the margarine in a bowl and beat until soft. Add 115 g/4 oz/½ cup of the caster sugar and continue to beat until the mixture is smooth and creamy.

2 Beat in the eggs, flour, baking powder, half the lemon rind and all the lemon juice. Stand 18 small paper cases in two bun tins, and divide the mixture among them.

3 Whisk the egg whites in a grease-free bowl, until they stand in soft peaks. Stir in the remaining caster sugar and grated lemon rind.

4 Put a spoonful of the meringue mixture on top of each cake. Cook for 20–25 minutes, until the meringue is crisp and brown. Serve hot or cold.

COOK'S TIP

Make sure that you whisk the egg whites enough before adding the sugar – when you lift out the whisk they should stand in peaks that just flop over slightly at the top. Use a mixture of oranges and lemons, for a sweeter taste.

Sticky Gingerbread Loaf

Moist and sticky, this classic gingerbread loaf is delicious with the tart lemon glacé icing drizzled over the top.

Makes 1 loaf

INGREDIENTS

175 g/6 oz/1½ cups plain flour
10 ml/2 tsp ground ginger
2.5 ml/½ tsp ground mixed spice
2.5 ml/½ tsp bicarbonate of soda
30 ml/2 tbsp black treacle
30 ml/2 tbsp golden syrup
75 g/3 oz/⅓ cup soft dark
   brown sugar
75 g/3 oz/6 tbsp butter
1 egg
15 ml/1 tbsp milk
15 ml/1 tbsp orange juice
2 pieces stem ginger, finely chopped
50 g/2 oz/⅓ cup sultanas
5 ready-to-eat dried apricots,
   finely chopped
45 ml/3 tbsp icing sugar
10 ml/2 tsp lemon juice

1 Preheat the oven to 160°C/325°F/ Gas 3. Grease and line a 1 kg/2¼ lb loaf tin. Sift the plain flour, mixed spices and bicarbonate of soda into a bowl. Place the black treacle, syrup, sugar and butter in a pan and heat gently until the butter has melted.

2 In a separate bowl, beat the egg, milk and orange juice together. Add the syrup mixture, egg mixture, chopped stem ginger, sultanas and apricots to the dry ingredients and stir to combine thoroughly.

butter
golden syrup
ground mixed spice
egg
milk
soft dark brown sugar
icing sugar
apricots
ground ginger
bicarbonate of soda
stem ginger
orange juice
black treacle
plain flour
sultanas
lemon juice

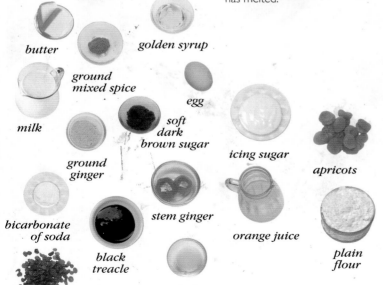

3 Spoon into the prepared tin and level out. Bake in the oven for about 50 minutes, or until the gingerbread is well risen, firm when touched gently in the centre and cooked through.

4 Leave the loaf to cool in the tin, then transfer to a wire rack. Mix the icing sugar with the lemon juice in a bowl and beat until smooth. Drizzle the icing back and forth over the top of the gingerbread, leave to set, then cut into thick slices to serve.

Chocolate and Banana Brownies

Nuts traditionally give brownies their chewy texture. Here oat bran is used instead, creating a moist, moreish yet healthy alternative.

Makes 9

INGREDIENTS
75 ml/5 tbsp cocoa powder
15 ml/1 tbsp caster sugar
75 ml/5 tbsp milk
3 large bananas, mashed
175 g/6 oz/1 cup soft light
  brown sugar
5 ml/1 tsp vanilla essence
5 egg whites
75 g/3 oz/¾ cup self-raising flour
75 g/3 oz/¾ cup oat bran
15 ml/1 tbsp icing sugar, for dusting

cocoa powder

caster sugar

vanilla essence

self-raising flour

milk

egg

icing sugar

soft light brown sugar

bananas

oat bran

COOK'S TIP

Store these brownies in an airtight tin for a day before eating – they improve with keeping.

1 Preheat the oven to 180°C/350°F/Gas 4. Line a 20 cm/8 in square tin with non-stick baking paper.

2 Blend the cocoa powder and caster sugar with the milk until smooth. Add the mashed bananas, soft brown sugar and vanilla essence.

3 Lightly beat the egg whites with a fork. Add the chocolate mixture and continue to beat well. Sift the flour over the mixture and fold in with the oat bran. Pour into the prepared tin.

4 Bake for 40 minutes or until firm. Cool the bake in the tin for 10 minutes, then turn out on to a wire rack. Cut into squares and dust lightly with icing sugar before serving.

Marbled Brownies

Swirling a rich cream cheese mixture through a chocolate-and-nut base makes for an absolutely irresistible combination.

Makes 24

INGREDIENTS
225 g/8 oz plain chocolate
75 g/3 oz/6 tbsp butter
4 eggs
350 g/12 oz/1½ cups sugar
115 g/4 oz/1 cup plain flour
2.5 ml/½ tsp salt
5 ml/1 tsp baking powder
10 ml/2 tsp vanilla essence
115 g/4 oz/1 cup walnuts, chopped

FOR THE PLAIN MIXTURE
50 g/2 oz/4 tbsp butter, at room
  temperature
115 g/4 oz/½ cup cream cheese
75 g/3 oz/¾ cup icing sugar
2 eggs
30 ml/2 tbsp plain flour
5 ml/1 tsp vanilla essence

icing sugar vanilla essence walnuts
butter

eggs plain flour
sugar baking powder
plain chocolate cream cheese
salt

1 Preheat the oven to 180°C/350°F/ Gas 4. Grease and line a 33 x 23 cm/ 13 x 9 in baking tin. Melt the chocolate and butter in a pan over a very low heat, stirring constantly. Set aside to cool.

2 Meanwhile, beat the eggs until light and fluffy. Gradually add the sugar and continue beating until blended. Sift over the flour, salt and baking powder and fold to combine.

3 Stir in the cooled chocolate mixture. Add the vanilla essence and walnuts. Measure and set aside 475 ml/16 fl oz/2 cups of the chocolate mixture.

4 For the plain mixture, cream the butter and cream cheese with an electric mixer. Add the sugar and continue beating until blended. Beat in the eggs, flour and vanilla essence.

5 Spread the unmeasured chocolate mixture in the tin. Pour over the cream cheese mixture. Drop spoonfuls of the reserved chocolate mixture on top.

6 With a metal spatula, swirl the mixtures to marble. Do not blend completely. Bake for 35–40 minutes, until just set. Remove from the tin when cool and leave on a wire rack until completely cold before cutting into squares for serving.

COOK'S TIP

For very fine or delicate marbling, use a metal skewer.

Spiced Honey Nut Cake

A combination of ground pistachio nuts and breadcrumbs replaces the flour in this recipe, resulting in a light, moist sponge cake. The unusual mixture of pistachio, lemon and cinnamon is mouth-watering.

Serves 8

INGREDIENTS
4 eggs, separated
115 g/4 oz/½ cup caster sugar
grated rind and juice of 1 lemon
150 g/5 oz/1¼ cups ground
    pistachio nuts
50 g/2 oz/¾ cup dried breadcrumbs

FOR THE SYRUP
1 lemon
90 ml/6 tbsp clear honey
1 cinnamon stick, broken
15 ml/1 tbsp brandy

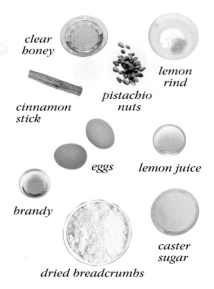

clear
honey

lemon
rind

pistachio
nuts

cinnamon
stick

eggs   lemon juice

brandy

caster
sugar

dried breadcrumbs

1 Preheat the oven to 180°C/350°F/ Gas 4. Grease and base-line a 20 cm/8 in square cake tin. Beat the egg yolks, sugar, lemon rind and juice together until pale and creamy. Fold in 115 g/4 oz/1 cup of the ground pistachio nuts and all the breadcrumbs.

2 In a grease-free bowl, whisk the egg whites until stiff, then fold into the creamed mixture. Transfer to the prepared tin and bake for 45 minutes, until risen and springy to the touch. Remove from the oven, cool in the tin for 10 minutes, then transfer to a wire rack to cool completely before decorating.

3 Meanwhile, to make the syrup, peel the lemon and cut the rind into very thin strips. Squeeze the juice into a small pan and add the honey and cinnamon stick. Bring to the boil, add the shredded rind, and simmer rapidly for 1 minute. Cool slightly and stir in the brandy.

4 Place the cold cake on a serving plate, prick all over with a skewer and pour over the cooled syrup, lemon shreds and lengths of cinnamon stick.

5 Sprinkle over the reserved pistachio nuts. Remove the pieces of cinnamon stick from individual slices, as they are purely for decoration.

Spiced Apple Cake

Grated apple and chopped dates give this cake a natural sweetness – omit 25 g/1 oz/2 tbsp of the sugar if the fruit is very sweet.

Serves 8

INGREDIENTS
225 g/8 oz/2 cups self-raising wholemeal flour
5 ml/1 tsp baking powder
10 ml/2 tsp ground cinnamon
175 g/6 oz/1 cup chopped dates
75 g/3 oz/½ cup light muscovado sugar
15 ml/1 tbsp pear and apple spread
120 ml/4 fl oz/½ cup apple juice
2 eggs
90 ml/6 tbsp sunflower oil
2 eating apples, cored and grated
15 ml/1 tbsp chopped walnuts

ground cinnamon

eggs

sunflower oil

apple juice

self-raising wholemeal flour

chopped dates

chopped walnuts

baking powder

muscovado sugar

pear and apple spread

eating apples

1 Preheat the oven to 180°C/350°F/ Gas 4. Grease and line a deep round 20 cm/8 in cake tin. Sift the flour, baking powder and cinnamon into a mixing bowl, then mix in the dates and make a well in the centre.

2 Mix the sugar with the pear and apple spread in a small bowl. Gradually stir in the apple juice. Add to the dry ingredients with the eggs, oil and apples. Mix thoroughly.

3 Spoon the mixture into the prepared cake tin, sprinkle with the walnuts and bake for 60–65 minutes or until a skewer inserted into the centre of the cake comes out clean. Transfer to a wire rack, remove the lining paper and leave to cool.

COOK'S TIP
It is not necessary to peel the apples – the skin adds extra fibre and softens on cooking.

Irish Whiskey Cake

This moist rich fruit cake is drizzled with whiskey as soon as it comes out of the oven.

Serves 12

INGREDIENTS
115 g/4 oz/⅔ cup glacé cherries
175 g/6 oz/1 cup dark muscovado
    sugar
115 g/4 oz/⅔ cup sultanas
115 g/4 oz/⅔ cup raisins
115 g/4 oz/⅔ cup currants
300 ml/½ pint/1¼ cups cold tea
300 g/11 oz/2½ cups self-raising
    flour, sifted
1 egg
45 ml/3 tbsp Irish whiskey

raisins

sultanas

currants

Irish
whiskey

dark
muscovado
sugar

egg

glacé
cherries

self-raising
flour

cold tea

1 Mix the cherries, sugar, dried fruit and tea in a large bowl. Leave to soak overnight until all the tea has been absorbed by the fruit.

2 Preheat the oven to 180°C/350°F/ Gas 4. Grease and line a 1 kg/2¼ lb loaf tin. Add the flour, then the egg to the fruit mixture and beat thoroughly until well mixed.

COOK'S TIP

If time is short, use hot tea and soak the fruit for just 2 hours.

3 Pour the mixture into the prepared tin and bake for 1½ hours or until a skewer inserted into the centre of the cake comes out clean.

4 Prick the top of the cake with a skewer and drizzle over the whiskey while the cake is still hot. Allow to stand for about 5 minutes, then remove from the tin and cool on a wire rack.

Sponge Cake with Fruit and Cream

Genoese is the French cake used as the base for both simple and elaborate creations. You could simply dust it with icing sugar, or layer it with seasonal fruits to serve with tea.

Serves 6

INGREDIENTS
115 g/4 oz/1 cup plain flour
pinch of salt
4 eggs, at room temperature
115 g/4 oz/½ cup caster sugar
2.5 ml/½ tsp vanilla essence
50 g/2 oz/4 tbsp butter, melted or
    clarified and cooled

FOR THE FILLING
450 g/1 lb fresh strawberries
30–60 ml/2–4 tbsp caster sugar
475 ml/16fl oz/2 cups whipping
    cream
5 ml/1 tsp vanilla essence

strawberries

eggs

butter

whipping cream

plain flour

vanilla essence *caster sugar*

1 Preheat the oven to 180°C/350°F/ Gas 4. Lightly butter a 23 cm/9 in springform tin or deep cake tin. Line the base with non-stick baking paper, and dust lightly with flour. Sift the flour and salt together twice.

2 Half-fill a medium saucepan with hot water and set over a low heat (do not allow the water to boil). Break the eggs into a heatproof bowl which just fits into the pan without touching the water. Using an electric mixer, beat the eggs at medium-high speed, gradually adding the sugar, for 8–10 minutes until the mixture is very thick and pale and leaves a ribbon trail when the beaters are lifted. Remove the bowl from the pan, add the vanilla essence and continue beating until the mixture is cool.

3 Fold in the flour mixture in three batches, using a balloon whisk or metal spoon. Before the third addition of flour, stir a large spoonful of the cake mixture into the melted or clarified butter, then fold the butter mixture into the remaining mixture with the last addition of flour. Work quickly, but gently, so the mixture does not deflate. Pour into the prepared tin, smoothing the top so the sides are slightly higher than the centre.

4 Bake for about 25–30 minutes until the top of the cake springs back when touched and the edge begins to shrink away from the sides of the tin. Place the cake in its tin on a wire rack to cool for 5–10 minutes, then invert the cake on to the rack and leave to cool completely. Peel off the paper.

5 To make the filling, slice the strawberries, place in a bowl, sprinkle with 15–30 ml/1–2 tbsp of the sugar and set aside. Beat the cream with enough of the remaining sugar to sweeten it to your taste. Beat in the vanilla essence until the cream holds soft peaks: do not overbeat.

6 To assemble the cake, split the sponge in half horizontally, using a serrated knife. Place the top, cut side up, on a serving plate. Spread with a third of the cream and cover with a layer of sliced strawberries. Place the bottom half of the cake, cut side down, on top of the filling and press lightly. Spread the remaining cream over the top and sides of the cake. Chill and serve with the remaining strawberries.

Spiced Carrot and Courgette Cake

If you can't resist the lure of a slice of iced cake, you'll love this moist, spiced sponge with its delicious creamy topping.

Serves 10

INGREDIENTS
1 medium carrot
1 medium courgette
3 eggs, separated
115 g/4 oz/⅔ cup soft light
    brown sugar
30 ml/2 tbsp ground almonds
finely grated rind of 1 orange
115 g/4 oz/1 cup self-raising
    wholemeal flour
5 ml/1 tsp ground cinnamon
5 ml/1 tsp icing sugar, for dusting
fondant carrots and courgettes,
    to decorate

FOR THE TOPPING
175 g/6 oz/¾ cup low-fat soft cheese
5 ml/1 tsp clear honey

egg

ground cinnamon

self-raising wholemeal flour

ground almonds

icing sugar

low-fat soft cheese

soft light brown sugar

orange

clear honey

courgette and carrot

1 Preheat the oven to 180°C/350°F/ Gas 4. Line an 18 cm/7 in square tin with non-stick baking paper. Coarsely grate the carrot and courgette.

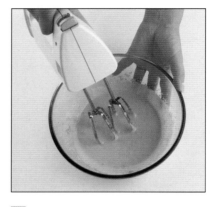

2 Put the egg yolks, sugar, ground almonds and orange rind into a bowl and whisk until very thick and light.

3 Sift the flour and cinnamon together and fold into the mixture with the grated vegetables. Add any bran left from the flour in the sieve.

4 Whisk the egg whites until stiff and carefully fold them in, half at a time. Spoon into the prepared tin. Bake in the oven for 1 hour, covering the top with foil after 40 minutes.

5 Leave to cool in the tin for about 5 minutes, then turn out on to a wire rack and carefully remove the non-stick lining paper.

6 For the topping, beat together the cheese and honey and spread over the cake. Decorate with fondant carrots and courgettes.

Peach Swiss Roll

A feather-light sponge enclosing peach jam, this would be delicious at tea-time.

Serves 6–8

INGREDIENTS
3 eggs
115 g/4 oz/½ cup caster sugar, plus
    extra for dusting
75 g/3 oz/¾ cup plain flour, sifted
90 ml/6 tbsp peach jam
icing sugar, for dusting (optional)

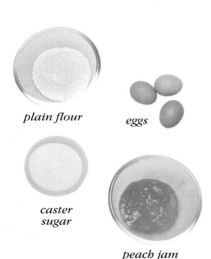

plain flour

eggs

*caster
sugar*

peach jam

1 Preheat the oven to 200°C/400°F/ Gas 6. Grease a 30 x 20 cm/12 x 8 in Swiss roll tin and line with non-stick baking paper. Combine the eggs and sugar in a bowl. Beat with a hand-held electric whisk until thick and mousse-like (when the whisk is lifted a trail should remain on the surface of the mixture for at least 15 seconds).

2 Carefully fold in the flour with a large metal spoon, then add 15 ml/ 1 tbsp boiling water in the same way.

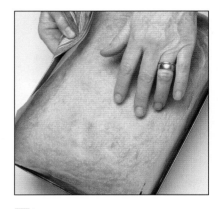

3 Spoon into the prepared tin, spread evenly to the edges and bake for about 10–12 minutes until the cake springs back when lightly pressed.

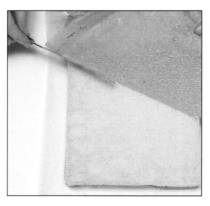

4 Spread a sheet of greaseproof paper on a flat surface, sprinkle it with caster sugar, then invert the cake on top. Peel off the lining paper.

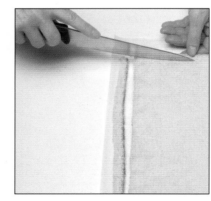

5 Neatly trim the edges of the cake. Make a neat cut two-thirds of the way through the cake, about 1 cm/½ in from the short edge nearest you.

6 Spread the cake with the peach jam and roll up quickly from the partially cut end. Hold in position for a minute, making sure the join is underneath. Cool on a wire rack. Decorate with glacé icing or simply dust with icing sugar before serving.

COOK'S TIP

Decorate the Swiss roll with glacé icing (see Basic Icings section). Put 115 g/4 oz glacé icing in a piping bag fitted with a small writing nozzle and pipe lines over the top of the Swiss roll.

Almond and Raspberry Swiss Roll

A light and airy whisked sponge cake is rolled up with a fresh cream and raspberry filling, making a classic Swiss roll.

Serves 8

INGREDIENTS
3 eggs
50 g/2 oz/¼ cup caster sugar, plus
    extra for dusting
50 g/2 oz/½ cup plain flour
25 g/1 oz/2 tbsp ground almonds
250 ml/8 fl oz/1 cup double cream
225 g/8 oz/1⅓ cups fresh raspberries
toasted flaked almonds,
    to decorate

double cream

plain flour

raspberries

eggs

caster sugar

flaked almonds

ground almonds

1 Preheat the oven to 200°C/400°F/ Gas 6. Grease a 33 × 23 cm/13 × 9 in Swiss roll tin and line with non-stick baking paper.

2 Whisk together the eggs and sugar in a heatproof bowl until thoroughly blended. Place the bowl over a saucepan of simmering water and whisk until thick and pale. Remove the bowl from the saucepan and continue whisking until the mixture is cool and leaves a thick trail on the surface when the beaters are lifted.

3 Sift the flour on to the surface, add the almonds and, using a plastic spatula, carefully fold into the mixture until smooth. Pour into the prepared tin, level, and bake for 10–12 minutes.

4 Place a sheet of greaseproof paper over a dish towel and sprinkle with caster sugar. Turn out the cake on to the sheet, and leave to cool with the tin in place. Remove the tin and carefully peel away the lining paper.

5 Reserve a little of the double cream for decoration, and whip the rest until it holds its shape. Fold in all but eight raspberries and spread the mixture over the cooled cake, leaving a narrow border around the edge.

6 Carefully roll the cake up from a narrow end. Sprinkle with caster sugar. Whip the remaining cream and pipe or spoon it along the centre of the roulade. Decorate with the reserved raspberries and toasted almonds.

Autumn Cake

This attractive cake is a wonderful way of using plentiful seasonal fruit.

Serves 6–8

INGREDIENTS
115 g/4 oz/½ cup butter, softened
150 g/5 oz/⅔ cup caster sugar
3 eggs, beaten
75 g/3 oz/1 cup ground hazelnuts
150 g/5 oz/1¼ cups shelled pecan
    nuts, chopped
50 g/2 oz/½ cup plain flour
5 ml/1 tsp baking powder
2.5 ml/½ tsp salt
675 g/1½ lb stoned plums
60 ml/4 tbsp lime marmalade
15 ml/1 tbsp lime juice
30 ml/2 tbsp chopped almonds,
    to decorate

eggs

lime　*plain flour*

butter

almonds

caster sugar

pecan nuts

salt

baking powder　*ground hazelnuts*

plums

1 Preheat the oven to 180°C/350°F/Gas 4. Grease a 23 cm/9 in round, fluted tart tin. Beat the butter and sugar until light and fluffy. Gradually beat in the eggs, alternating with the ground hazelnuts. Stir in the pecans, then sift in the flour, baking powder and salt. Fold in evenly.

2 Transfer the mixture to the prepared tin and bake for 45–50 minutes or until a skewer inserted into the centre comes out clean.

3 Remove from the oven and carefully arrange the fruit on top. Return to the oven and bake for 10–15 minutes more until the fruit has softened. Transfer to a wire rack to cool completely, then remove the cake from the tin.

4 Place the marmalade and lime juice in a small saucepan and warm gently. Brush over the fruit, then sprinkle with the almonds. Allow to set, then chill before serving.

COOK'S TIP

Use greengages or semi-dried prunes instead of plums, if you like.

Apple Crumble Cake

In the autumn use windfall apples. Served warm with thick cream or custard, this cake doubles as a delectable dessert.

Serves 8–10

INGREDIENTS
50 g/2 oz/4 tbsp butter, softened
75 g/3 oz/6 tbsp caster sugar
1 egg, beaten
115 g/4 oz/1 cup self-raising flour, sifted
2 cooking apples, peeled, cored and sliced
50 g/2 oz/⅓ cup sultanas

FOR THE TOPPING
75 g/3 oz/¾ cup self-raising flour
2.5 ml/½ tsp ground cinnamon
40 g/1½ oz/3 tbsp butter
25 g/1 oz/2 tbsp caster sugar

TO DECORATE
1 red dessert apple, cored, thinly sliced and tossed in lemon juice
25 g/1 oz/2 tbsp caster sugar, sifted
pinch of ground cinnamon

dessert apple
butter
sultanas
cooking apples
egg
lemon
self-raising flour
cinnamon
caster sugar

1 Preheat the oven to 180°C/350°F/ Gas 4. Grease and base-line a deep 18 cm/7 in springform tin. Put the butter, sugar, egg and flour into a bowl and beat for 1–2 minutes until smooth. Spoon into the prepared tin.

2 Make the topping. Sift the flour and cinnamon into a mixing bowl. Rub the butter in until the mixture resembles breadcrumbs, then stir in the sugar. Set aside.

3 Mix together the apple slices and sultanas and spread them evenly over the top of the cake mixture. Sprinkle the topping evenly over the surface.

4 Bake the cake for about 1 hour. Cool in the tin for 10 minutes before turning out on to a wire rack and peeling off the lining paper. Serve warm or cool, decorated with slices of red dessert apple and with caster sugar and cinnamon sprinkled over.

COOK'S TIP
Streusel topping – the crumble mixture – is delicious on a cake. Try using pears instead of apples and add a pinch of ground cardamom to the topping.

Banana Lemon Layer Cake

Banana loaf is a favourite teabread. Here is its more sophisticated cousin.

Serves 8–10

INGREDIENTS
250 g/9 oz/2¼ cups plain flour
7.5 ml/1½ tsp baking powder
2.5 ml/½ tsp salt
115 g/4 oz/½ cup butter, softened
225 g/8 oz/1 cup granulated sugar
75 g/3 oz/⅓ cup soft light
   brown sugar
2 eggs
2.5 ml/½ tsp grated lemon rind
2 very ripe bananas, mashed
5 ml/1 tsp vanilla essence
60 ml/4 tbsp milk
75 g/3 oz/¾ cup chopped walnuts
pared lemon rind, to decorate

FOR THE ICING
115 g/4 oz/½ cup butter, softened
500 g/1¼ lb/5 cups icing sugar
5 ml/1 tsp grated lemon rind
45–75 ml/3–5 tbsp lemon juice

vanilla essence
baking powder
lemon juice
soft light brown sugar
butter
granulated sugar
lemon rind
plain flour
eggs
milk
bananas
walnuts

1 Preheat the oven to 180°C/350°F/ Gas 4. Grease and base-line two 23cm/ 9 in round cake tins. Sift the flour with the baking powder and salt.

2 Cream the butter with the sugars until light and fluffy. Beat in the eggs, then stir in the grated lemon rind.

3 In a small bowl mix the mashed bananas with the vanilla essence and milk. Add the banana mixture and the dry ingredients to the butter mixture alternately in two or three batches and stir until just blended. Fold in the nuts.

4 Divide the mixture between the cake tins and spread it out evenly. Bake for 30–35 minutes or until a skewer inserted into one of the cakes comes out clean. Allow to stand for 5 minutes before turning out on a wire rack. Peel off the lining paper.

5 Make the icing. Cream the butter until smooth, then gradually beat in the icing sugar. Stir in the lemon rind and enough juice to make a spreadable consistency.

6 Put one of the cake layers on a serving plate. Cover with about one-third of the icing. Top with the second cake layer. Spread the remaining icing evenly over the cake and decorate with the pared lemon rind.

Custard Layer Cake

A creamy custard makes the perfect filling for a layer cake, and chocolate icing provides the perfect topping.

Serves 8

INGREDIENTS
225 g/8 oz/2 cups plain flour
15 ml/1 tbsp baking powder
pinch of salt
115 g/4 oz/½ cup butter, softened
225 g/8 oz/1 cup caster sugar
2 eggs
5 ml/1 tsp vanilla essence
175 ml/6 fl oz/¾ cup milk

FOR THE FILLING
3 egg yolks
115 g/4 oz /½ cup caster sugar
25 g/1 oz/¼ cup plain flour
250 ml/8 fl oz/1 cup hot milk
15 g/½ oz/1 tbsp butter
15 ml/1 tbsp brandy

FOR THE CHOCOLATE ICING
25 g/1 oz plain chocolate
25 g/1 oz/2 tbsp butter
50 g/2 oz/½ cup icing sugar, plus
    extra for dusting
2.5 ml/½ tsp vanilla essence
about 15 ml/1 tbsp hot water

vanilla essence

brandy

butter

icing sugar

plain chocolate

eggs

milk

caster sugar

baking powder

plain flour

1 Preheat the oven to 190°C/375°F/ Gas 5. Grease and base-line two deep round cake tins. Sift together the flour, baking powder and salt.

2 Beat the butter and caster sugar until light and fluffy. Add the eggs one at a time, beating well. Stir in the vanilla essence. Add the milk and dry ingredients alternately, mixing only enough to blend thoroughly.

3 Divide the cake mixture between the prepared tins and smooth the top evenly. Bake for about 25 minutes, until a skewer inserted in the centre of one of the cakes comes out clean.

4 Make the filling. Whisk the egg yolks in a heatproof mixing bowl. Gradually add the sugar and continue whisking until the mixture is thick and pale yellow. Beat in the flour, then pour in the hot milk in a steady stream, beating constantly.

5 Place the bowl over a pan of boiling water. Heat, stirring constantly, until thickened. Cook for a further 2 minutes, then turn off the heat. Stir in the butter and brandy. Set aside until cold, stirring frequently.

6 When the cakes have completely cooled, place one on a serving plate and carefully spread over the custard filling in a thick layer using a large palette knife. Place the other cake on top.

7 To make the icing, melt the chocolate with the butter in a heatproof bowl set over a pan of hot water. When smooth, remove from the heat and beat in the icing sugar and vanilla essence, then beat in enough hot water to make a spreadable consistency. Spread the icing evenly over the top of the cake. Dust with icing sugar.

COOK'S TIP
Give the custard filling a touch of luxury by stirring in about 15 ml/ 1 tbsp orange-flavoured liqueur. Grand Marnier is excellent and the flavoured custard tastes good with the chocolate icing.

Kugelhopf

Guaranteed to rise to the occasion, this fruit-and-nut bread looks as good as it tastes.

Makes 1 loaf

INGREDIENTS
115 g/4 oz/⅔ cup raisins
15 ml/1 tbsp kirsch or brandy
1 sachet dried yeast
60 ml/4 tbsp lukewarm water
115 g/4 oz/½ cup unsalted butter,
    at room temperature
115 g/4 oz/½ cup sugar
3 eggs, at room temperature
grated rind of 1 lemon
5 ml/1 tsp salt
2.5 ml/½ tsp vanilla essence
350 g/12 oz/3 cups flour
120 ml/4 fl oz/½ cup milk
25 g/1 oz/¼ cup slivered almonds
50 g/2 oz/½ cup blanched almonds,
    chopped
icing sugar, for dusting

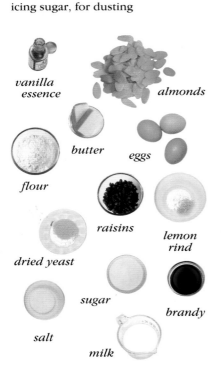

vanilla
essence   almonds

butter   eggs

flour

raisins

dried yeast   lemon
                   rind

sugar

salt   brandy

milk

1 In a bowl, combine the raisins and kirsch or brandy. Set aside. Combine the yeast and water, stir and leave for 5 minutes until frothy.

2 With an electric mixer, cream the butter and sugar until thick and fluffy. Beat in the eggs, one at a time. Add the lemon rind, salt and vanilla essence. Stir in the yeast mixture.

3 Add the flour, alternating with the milk, until the mixture is well blended. Cover and leave to rise in a warm place until doubled in volume, about 2 hours.

4 Grease a 2.4 litre/4 pint/10 cup kugelhopf tin, then sprinkle the slivered almonds evenly over the bottom.

5 Work the raisins and blanched almonds into the dough, then spoon into the tin. Cover with a plastic bag and leave to rise in a warm place for about 1 hour until the dough almost reaches the top of the tin. Preheat the oven to 180°C/350°F/Gas 4.

6 Bake for 45 minutes, or until golden brown. If the top browns too quickly, cover it with foil. Allow to cool in the tin for 15 minutes, then invert on to a rack. Dust the top lightly with icing sugar before serving.

Angel Cake

Serve this light-as-air cake with cream or fromage frais – it makes a tasty treat.

Serves 10

INGREDIENTS
40 g/1½ oz/⅓ cup cornflour
40 g/1½ oz/⅓ cup plain flour
8 egg whites
225 g/8 oz/1 cup caster sugar,
  plus extra for sprinkling
5 ml/1 tsp vanilla essence
icing sugar, for dusting

cornflour

vanilla essence

plain flour

caster sugar

eggs

1 Preheat the oven to 180°C/350°F/ Gas 4. Sift both flours on to a sheet of greaseproof paper.

2 Whisk the egg whites in a large grease-free bowl until very stiff, then gradually add the sugar and vanilla essence, whisking until the mixture is thick and glossy.

COOK'S TIP

Make a lemony icing by mixing 175 g/6 oz/1½ cups icing sugar with 15–30 ml/1–2 tbsp lemon juice. Drizzle the icing over the cake and decorate with physalis or lemon slices and mint sprigs.

3 Gently fold in the flour mixture with a large metal spoon. Spoon into an ungreased 25 cm/10 in angel cake tin, smooth the surface and bake for about 45–50 minutes, until the cake springs back when lightly pressed.

4 Sprinkle a piece of greaseproof paper with caster sugar and set an egg cup in the centre. Invert the cake tin over the paper, balancing it carefully on the egg cup. When cold, the cake will drop out of the tin. Transfer it to a plate, decorate if liked (see Cook's Tip), or dust with icing sugar and serve.

Savarin with Summer Fruit

This traditional dessert from Alsace-Lorraine is made from a rich yeast dough moistened with syrup and cherry liqueur.

Serves 10–12

INGREDIENTS
1 sachet dried yeast
50 g/2 oz/¼ cup caster sugar
60 ml/4 tbsp lukewarm water
275 g/10 oz/2½ cups plain flour
4 eggs, beaten
5 ml/1 tsp vanilla essence
90 g/3½ oz/7 tbsp unsalted butter,
    softened
450 g/1 lb fresh raspberries
mint leaves, to decorate
whipped cream, to serve

FOR THE SYRUP
225 g/8 oz/1 cup caster sugar
600 ml/1 pint/2½ cups water
90 ml/6 tbsp redcurrant jelly
45 ml/3 tbsp kirsch (optional)

caster sugar *eggs* *raspberries*
redcurrant jelly *plain flour* *kirsch*
mint leaves *butter* *vanilla essence* *whipped cream* *dried yeast*

1 Generously butter a 23 cm/9 in savarin or ring tin. Put the yeast and 15 ml/1 tbsp of the sugar in a medium bowl, add the water and stir until dissolved, then leave the yeast mixture to stand for about 5 minutes until frothy.

2 Put the flour and remaining sugar in a food processor and pulse to combine. With the machine running, slowly pour in the yeast mixture, eggs and vanilla essence, then scrape down the sides and continue processing until a soft dough forms. Add the butter and pulse until incorporated.

4 Place the tin on a baking sheet in the oven and reduce the temperature to 180°C/350°F/Gas 4. Bake for 25 minutes until the top is a rich golden colour and springs back when touched. Turn out the cake on to a wire rack and cool slightly.

COOK'S TIP

This is equally delicious with strawberries, or use a mixture of summer fruit. Redcurrants on the stem make a pretty decoration.

3 Place the dough in spoonfuls into the tin, leaving a space between each mound of dough (this will fill in as the dough rises). Tap the tin gently to release any air bubbles, then cover with a dish towel to rise for about 1 hour. The dough should double in bulk and come just to the top of the tin. Preheat the oven to 200°C/400°F/Gas 6.

5 To make the syrup, blend the sugar, water and 60 ml/4 tbsp of the redcurrant jelly in a saucepan. Bring to the boil over a medium-high heat, stirring until the sugar and jelly dissolve, and boil for 3 minutes.

6 Remove the syrup from the heat and allow to cool slightly, then stir in the kirsch, if using. In a small bowl, combine 30 ml/2 tbsp of the hot syrup with the remaining redcurrant jelly and stir to dissolve. Set aside.

7 Place the rack with the cake, still warm, over a baking tray. Slowly spoon the syrup over the cake, catching any extra syrup in the tray and spooning it over the cake, until all the syrup has been absorbed. Carefully transfer the cake to a shallow serving dish (the cake will be very fragile) and pour over any remaining syrup. Brush the redcurrant glaze over the top, then fill the centre with raspberries and decorate with mint leaves. Chill, then serve with the cream.

Simple Chocolate Cake

An easy, everyday chocolate cake which can be simply filled with chocolate butter icing, or pepped up with a rich chocolate ganache for a special occasion.

Serves 6–8

INGREDIENTS

115 g/4 oz plain chocolate, broken
   into squares
45 ml/3 tbsp milk
150 g/5 oz/⅔ cup unsalted butter or
   margarine, softened
150 g/5 oz/scant 1 cup light
   muscovado sugar
3 eggs
200 g/7 oz/1¾ cups self-raising flour
15 ml/1 tbsp cocoa powder
1 quantity Chocolate Butter Icing,
   for the filling, see Basic Icings
icing sugar and cocoa powder, for
   dusting

eggs

plain chocolate

milk

icing sugar

butter

cocoa powder

self-raising flour

light muscovado sugar

1 Preheat the oven to 180°C/350°F/ Gas 4. Grease two 18 cm/7 in round sandwich cake tins and line the base of each with non-stick baking paper. Melt the chocolate with the milk in a heatproof bowl set over a pan of simmering water.

2 Cream the butter or margarine with the sugar in a mixing bowl until pale and fluffy. Add the eggs one at a time, beating well after each addition. Stir in the chocolate mixture and mix until thoroughly combined.

COOK'S TIP

For a richer finish, make a double quantity of butter icing and spread or pipe over the top of the cake as well as using for the filling.

3 Sift the flour and cocoa over the mixture and fold in with a metal spoon until evenly mixed. Scrape into the prepared tins, smooth level and bake for 35–40 minutes or until well risen and firm. Turn out on to wire racks to cool.

4 Sandwich the cake layers together with the butter icing. Dust with a mixture of icing sugar and cocoa just before serving.

Chocolate Layer Cake

The cake layers can be made ahead, wrapped and frozen for future use. Always thaw cakes completely before icing.

Serves 10–12

INGREDIENTS

225 g/8 oz can cooked whole
  beetroot, drained and
  juice reserved
115 g/4 oz/½ cup butter, softened
500 g/1¼ lb/2½ cups soft light
  brown sugar
3 eggs
15 ml/1 tbsp vanilla essence
75 g/3 oz plain chocolate, melted
225 g/8 oz/2 cups plain flour
10 ml/2 tsp baking powder
2.5 ml/½ tsp salt
120 ml/4 fl oz/½ cup buttermilk
chocolate curls (optional)

FOR THE GANACHE

475 ml/16 fl oz/2 cups whipping or
  double cream
450 g/1 lb bittersweet chocolate,
  chopped
15 ml/1 tbsp vanilla essence

vanilla essence

beetroot

cocoa powder

butter

eggs

light brown sugar

bittersweet chocolate

buttermilk

chocolate curls

cream

baking powder

salt

flour

plain chocolate

1 Preheat the oven to 180°C/350°F/ Gas 4. Grease two 23 cm/9 in cake tins. Grate the beetroot and add to the reserved juice. Beat the butter, brown sugar, eggs and vanilla essence until pale and fluffy. Beat in the chocolate.

2 Beat in the flour, baking powder and salt, alternately with the buttermilk. Add the beetroot mixture and beat for 1 minute. Divide between the tins and bake for 30–35 minutes. Cool slightly, then turn out and cool completely.

3 Make the ganache. In a heavy-based saucepan over a medium heat, bring the cream to the boil, stirring occasionally. Remove from the heat and stir in the chocolate, stirring constantly until melted and smooth. Stir in the vanilla essence. Strain into a bowl and refrigerate, stirring every 10 minutes, until spreadable: this will take about 1 hour.

4 Assemble the cake. Place one layer on a serving plate and spread with one-third of the ganache. Top with the remaining cake layer bottom side up and spread the remaining ganache over the top and sides. If using, decorate with the chocolate curls. Allow the ganache to set for 20–30 minutes, then refrigerate before serving.

Chocolate Chestnut Roulade

For an alternative decoration, dip 12 glacéed chestnuts halfway into melted plain chocolate, allow to set and use to decorate the roulade.

Serves 10–12

INGREDIENTS
175 g/6 oz bittersweet chocolate, chopped
30 ml/2 tbsp sifted cocoa powder, plus extra for dusting
60 ml/4 tbsp strong coffee
6 eggs, separated
75 g/3 oz/6 tbsp caster sugar
pinch of cream of tartar
5 ml/1 tsp vanilla essence
glacéed chestnuts, to decorate

FOR THE CHESTNUT CREAM FILLING
475 ml/16 fl oz/2 cups double cream
15 ml/1 tbsp rum
350 g/12 oz/1½ cups canned sweetened chestnut purée
115 g/4 oz bittersweet chocolate, grated

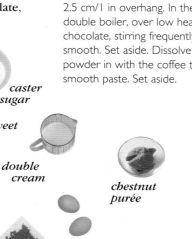

caster sugar

bittersweet chocolate

strong coffee

rum

double cream

glacéed chestnuts

chestnut purée

cream of tartar

eggs

cocoa powder

vanilla essence

1 Preheat the oven to 180°C/350°F/Gas 4. Grease a 39 x 27 x 2.5 cm/15½ x 10½ x 1 in Swiss roll tin. Base-line with non-stick baking paper, allowing 2.5 cm/1 in overhang. In the top of a double boiler, over low heat, melt the chocolate, stirring frequently until smooth. Set aside. Dissolve the cocoa powder in with the coffee to make a smooth paste. Set aside.

2 Beat the egg yolks with half the sugar until pale and thick. Slowly beat in the melted chocolate and cocoa paste until just blended.

3 Beat the egg whites and cream of tartar in a grease-free bowl until stiff peaks form. Sprinkle the remaining sugar over the whites in two batches and beat until stiff and glossy; beat in the vanilla essence. Stir a spoonful of the whites into the chocolate mixture to lighten it, then fold in the remaining whites. Spoon into the prepared tin. Bake for 20–25 minutes or until the cake springs back when touched with a fingertip.

4 Meanwhile, dust a dish towel with cocoa. Turn out the cake on to the towel and remove the paper. Starting at a narrow end, roll up cake and towel together. Cool completely.

5 Prepare the filling. Whip the cream and rum until soft peaks form. Beat a spoonful of cream into the chestnut purée to lighten it, then fold in the remaining cream and grated chocolate. Reserve a quarter of the chestnut cream mixture for the decoration.

COOK'S TIP
Beating egg whites should always be the last step in the preparation of cakes or any other recipes. Once beaten, egg whites should be folded in immediately and never held.

6 Assemble the roulade. Unroll the cake and, if you like, trim the edges. Spread the chestnut cream mixture to within 2.5 cm/1 in of the edge of the cake. Using the towel to lift the cake, gently roll it up, Swiss roll fashion.

7 Place the roulade seam-side down on a serving plate. Spread the reserved chestnut cream over the top of the roulade; spoon some into a small icing bag fitted with a medium star tip. Pipe rosettes down the sides of the roulade. Decorate with glacéed chestnuts.

Sachertorte

One of the world's finest – and most famous –
cakes, Sachertorte is dark and delectable.

Serves 8–10

INGREDIENTS
50 g/2 oz plain chocolate
50 g/2 oz dark chocolate
75 g/3 oz/6 tbsp butter, softened
115 g/4 oz/½ cup granulated sugar
4 eggs, separated, plus 1 egg white
1.5 ml/¼ tsp salt
50 g/2 oz/½ cup plain flour, sifted

FOR THE TOPPING
75 g/3 oz/5 tbsp apricot jam
250 ml/8 fl oz/1 cup water plus
   15 ml/1 tbsp extra
15 g/½ oz/1 tbsp butter
175 g/6 oz dark chocolate
175 g/6 oz/¾ cup granulated sugar
ready-made chocolate decorating
   icing (optional)

apricot jam

dark
chocolate

salt

butter

granulated
sugar

eggs

plain
chocolate

plain flour

1 Preheat the oven to 160°C/325°F/
Gas 3. Line and grease a 23 cm/9 in
round cake tin. Melt both chocolates
in the top of a double boiler, or in
a heatproof bowl set over hot water.
Set aside.

2 In a mixing bowl, cream the butter and sugar until light and fluffy. Stir in the
chocolate, then beat in the egg yolks, one at a time.

3 In a grease-free bowl, beat the egg
whites with the salt until stiff. Fold a
dollop of whites into the chocolate
mixture to lighten it. Fold in the
remaining whites in three batches,
alternating with the sifted flour.

4 Pour into the tin and bake for about
45 minutes, until a skewer, inserted in
the cake, comes out clean. Cool on
a wire rack.

5 Make the topping. Melt the jam with
15 ml/1 tbsp of the water over a low
heat, then strain for a smooth
consistency. In the top of a double boiler
or in a heatproof bowl set over hot
water, melt the butter and chocolate.

6 In a heavy saucepan, dissolve the sugar in the remaining water over a low heat. Raise the heat and boil until the mixture reaches 110°C/225°F on a sugar thermometer. Immediately plunge the bottom of the pan into cold water and leave for 1 minute. Pour into the chocolate mixture and stir to blend. Let the icing cool for a few minutes. Meanwhile, brush the warm jam over the cake. Starting in the centre, pour over the chocolate icing and work outward in a circular movement. Tilt the rack to spread; only use a spatula for the sides of the cake. Leave to set overnight. If wished, decorate with chocolate icing.

COOK'S TIP
Use unsalted butter for cake making – it really does make a difference to the flavour.

Mississippi Mud Cake

Dense, dark and dreamy, this is definitely a special-occasion cake.

Serves 8–10

INGREDIENTS

225 g/8 oz/2 cups plain flour
pinch of salt
5 ml/1 tsp baking powder
300 ml/½ pint/1¼ cups strong
　　black coffee
60 ml/4 tbsp brandy
150 g/5 oz chocolate
225 g/8 oz/1 cup butter
450 g/1 lb/2 cups granulated sugar
2 eggs, at room temperature
7.5 ml/1½ tsp vanilla essence
cocoa powder, for dusting
sweetened whipped cream,
　　to serve

chocolate

cocoa powder

brandy

butter

vanilla essence

baking powder

cream

eggs

granulated sugar

coffee

plain flour

1 Preheat the oven to 140°C/275°F/Gas 1. Grease a 3 litre/5 pint/12 cup bundt tin (see Cook's Tip, below). Dust it with cocoa powder. Sift the flour, salt and baking powder together.

2 Combine the coffee, brandy, chocolate and butter in the top of a double boiler. Heat until the chocolate and butter have melted and the mixture is smooth, stirring occasionally.

3 Pour the chocolate mixture into a large bowl. Using an electric mixer on low speed, gradually beat in the sugar until dissolved.

4 Raise the speed to medium and add the sifted dry ingredients. Mix well, then beat in the eggs and vanilla essence until thoroughly blended. Pour the batter into the tin and bake for 1¼–1½ hours or until a skewer, inserted in the cake, comes out clean.

COOK'S TIP
A bundt tin is a large fluted ring tin, also known as a kugelhopf tin. It is perfect for Mississippi Mud Cake, but you can use an angel cake tin instead.

5 Let the cake cool in the tin for 15 minutes, then turn it out on to a wire rack. Leave to cool completely, then transfer to a plate and dust lightly with cocoa powder. Serve with the sweetened whipped cream.

French Chocolate Cake

This is a typical French home-made cake – dark and delicious. The dense texture is very different from that of a sponge cake and it is excellent served with cream or a fruit *coulis*.

Serves 10–12

INGREDIENTS
150 g/5 oz/¾ cup caster sugar, plus
    extra for sprinkling
275 g/10 oz plain chocolate,
    chopped
175 g/6 oz/¾ cup unsalted butter,
    cut into pieces, plus extra
    for greasing
10 ml/2 tsp vanilla essence
5 eggs, separated
40 g/1½ oz/6 tbsp plain flour, sifted
pinch of salt
icing sugar, for dusting
sweetened whipped cream, to serve

cream

caster sugar

plain flour

icing sugar

vanilla essence

plain chocolate

butter

eggs

1 Preheat the oven to 160°C/325°F/ Gas 3. Generously butter a 24 cm/9½ in springform tin, then sprinkle the tin with a little sugar and tap out the excess.

2 Set aside 45 ml/3 tbsp of the sugar. Place the rest in a heavy-based saucepan with the chocolate and butter and cook over a low heat until the chocolate and butter have melted and the sugar has dissolved. Remove the pan from the heat, stir in the vanilla essence and leave the mixture to cool slightly.

3 Beat the egg yolks into the chocolate mixture, then stir in the flour. In a bowl, beat the egg whites until they are frothy. Add the salt and continue beating until soft peaks form. Sprinkle over the reserved sugar and beat until the whites are stiff and glossy. Beat one-third of the whites into the chocolate mixture, then fold in the remaining whites.

4 Carefully pour the mixture into the tin and tap the tin gently to release any air bubbles. Bake for 35–45 minutes until the cake has risen well and the top springs back when touched lightly with a fingertip. Cool the cake on a wire rack. Dust the cake with icing sugar and transfer to a serving plate. Serve with sweetened whipped cream.

Chocolate Banana Cake

A chocolate cake that's delightfully low-fat – it is moist enough to eat without the icing if you want to cut down on calories.

Serves 8

INGREDIENTS

225 g/8 oz/2 cups self-raising flour
45 ml/3 tbsp fat-reduced cocoa
    powder
115 g/4 oz/⅔ cup light muscovado
    sugar
30 ml/2 tbsp malt extract
30 ml/2 tbsp golden syrup
2 eggs
60 ml/4 tbsp skimmed milk
60 ml/4 tbsp sunflower oil
2 large ripe bananas, mashed

FOR THE ICING

225 g/8 oz/2 cups icing sugar, sifted
35 ml/7 tsp fat-reduced cocoa
    powder, sifted
15–30 ml/1–2 tbsp warm water

golden syrup
eggs
skimmed milk
icing sugar
self-raising flour
fat-reduced cocoa powder
sunflower oil
bananas
malt extract
light muscovado sugar

1 Preheat the oven to 160°C/325°F/ Gas 3. Grease and line a deep round 20 cm/8 in cake tin.

2 Sift the flour into a mixing bowl with the cocoa powder. Stir in the sugar.

3 Make a well in the centre and add the malt extract, golden syrup, eggs, milk and oil. Stir the bananas into the mixture until thoroughly combined.

4 Pour the cake mixture into the prepared tin and bake for 1–1¼ hours or until the centre of the cake springs back when lightly pressed.

5 Remove the cake from the tin and leave on a wire rack to cool.

COOK'S TIP

This cake also makes a delicious dessert if heated in the microwave. The icing melts to a puddle of sauce. Serve a slice topped with a large dollop of fromage frais for a really special treat.

6 Make the icing. Reserve 50 g/2 oz/½ cup icing sugar and 5 ml/1 tsp cocoa powder. Make a thick, dark icing by beating the remaining sugar and cocoa powder with a little warm water. Spread it over the top of the cake. Mix the reserved icing sugar and cocoa powder with a few drops of water to make a thin icing; drizzle this across the top of the cake to decorate.

White Chocolate Mousse and Strawberry Layer Cake

The strawberries in this cake can be replaced with raspberries or blackberries, complemented with a liqueur of the appropriate flavour.

Serves 10

INGREDIENTS
115 g/4 oz good-quality white
  chocolate, chopped
120 ml/4 fl oz/½ cup double cream
120 ml/4 fl oz/½ cup milk
15 ml/1 tbsp rum or vanilla essence
115 g/4 oz/½ cup butter, softened
175 g/6 oz/¾ cup granulated sugar
3 eggs
225 g/8 oz/2 cups plain flour
5 ml/1 tsp baking powder
pinch of salt
675 g/1½ lb fresh strawberries,
  sliced, plus extra to decorate
750 ml/1¼ pints/3 cups whipping
  cream
30 ml/2 tbsp rum or strawberry-
  flavoured liqueur

FOR THE MOUSSE FILLING
250 g/9 oz fine quality white
  chocolate, chopped
350 ml/12 fl oz/1½ cups whipping
  or double cream
30 ml/2 tbsp rum or strawberry-
  flavoured liqueur

1 Preheat the oven to 180°C/350°F/ Gas 4. Grease two 23 x 5 cm/9 x 2 in cake tins. Line the base of the tins with non-stick baking paper. Melt the chocolate and double cream in a double boiler over a low heat, stirring until smooth. Stir in the milk and rum or vanilla essence; set aside to cool.

2 In a large mixing bowl, beat the butter and sugar for 3–5 minutes until light and creamy, scraping the sides of the bowl occasionally. Add the eggs one at a time, beating well after each addition. In a small bowl, sift together the flour, baking powder and salt. Alternately add the flour and melted chocolate to the egg mixture, until just blended. Pour the mixture into the tins and spread evenly.

3 Bake for 20–25 minutes until a skewer inserted into the centre of one of the cakes comes out clean. Cool in the tins for 10 minutes. Turn the cakes out on to a wire rack, peel off the paper and cool completely.

4 Prepare the filling. Melt the chocolate in the cream over a low heat until smooth, stirring frequently. Stir in the rum or liqueur and pour into a bowl. Chill until the mixture is just set. With a wire whisk, whip lightly until the mixture is mousse-like.

cream
strawberries
eggs
butter
baking powder
plain flour
white chocolate
granulated sugar
liqueur
milk
vanilla essence

5 Slice both cake layers in half, making four layers. Place one layer on a plate and spread with one-third of the mousse. Arrange about one-third of the sliced strawberries over the mousse. Add two more layers in the same way, then cover with the last cake layer.

6 Whip the cream with the rum or liqueur. Spread about half the whipped cream over the top and sides of the cake. Use the remaining cream to pipe scrolls on top of the cake. Decorate with the remaining strawberries.

Death by Chocolate

There are many versions of this cake; here is a very rich one which is ideal for a large party.

Serves 18–20

INGREDIENTS
200 g/7 oz extra-fine plain
   chocolate, chopped
115 g/4 oz/½ cup butter, diced
150 ml/¼ pint/⅔ cup water
275 g/10 oz/1¼ cups granulated
   sugar
10 ml/2 tsp vanilla essence
2 eggs, separated
175 ml/6 fl oz/¾ cup soured cream
350 g/12 oz/3 cups plain flour
10 ml/2 tsp baking powder
5 ml/1 tsp bicarbonate of soda
chocolate curls, raspberries and
   icing sugar, to decorate

FOR THE FILLING AND GLAZE
600 g/1 lb 5 oz extra-fine plain
   chocolate, chopped
225 g/8 oz/1 cup butter
75ml/5 tbsp brandy
215 g/7½ oz/¾ cup seedless
   raspberry jam
250 ml/8 fl oz/1 cup double cream

brandy

eggs

chocolate curls

raspberry jam

baking powder

icing sugar

plain flour

granulated sugar

butter

soured cream

double cream

bicarbonate of soda

raspberries

vanilla essence

plain chocolate

1 Preheat the oven to 180°C/350°F/ Gas 4. Grease a 25 cm/10 in springform tin and base-line with non-stick baking paper. In a saucepan over a low heat, heat the chocolate, butter and water until melted, stirring. Remove from the heat, beat in the sugar and vanilla and cool. Beat the yolks lightly, then beat into the chocolate mixture; gently fold in the soured cream. Sift the flour, baking powder and bicarbonate of soda over, then fold in. Whisk the egg whites until stiff; fold into the chocolate mixture.

2 Pour the mixture into the tin and bake for 50–60 minutes until the cake begins to shrink away from the side of the tin. Put the tin on a wire rack to cool for 10 minutes (the cake may sink in the centre; this is normal). Run a sharp knife around the edge of the cake, then remove the side of the tin. Invert the cake on the rack, remove the base of the tin and cool completely. Wash and dry the tin.

3 Prepare the filling and glaze. Melt 400 g/14 oz of the chocolate with the butter and 60 ml/4 tbsp of the brandy. Cool, then chill until thickened. Cut the cake into three equal layers. Heat the raspberry jam and remaining brandy until melted and smooth, stirring. Spread a thin layer over each cake layer and allow to set.

4 When the filling is spreadable, place the bottom cake layer back in the tin. Spread with half the filling and top with the second layer of cake, then spread with the remaining filling; top with the final cake layer, jam side down. Gently press the layers together, cover and chill for 4–6 hours or overnight.

5 Run a knife around the edge of the cake, then remove the side of the tin. Set the cake on a wire rack over a baking sheet. Bring the cream to the boil. Remove from the heat and add the remaining chocolate, stirring until melted. Stir in the brandy and strain into a bowl. Leave to cool.

6 Whisk the chocolate mixture until it begins to hold its shape. Smooth it over the cake and leave to set. Slide the cake on to a serving plate and decorate with chocolate curls and raspberries. Dust with icing sugar. Serve at room temperature.

Chocolate Gâteau Terrine

A spectacular finale to a special-occasion meal. You'll find this is well worth the time and effort required to make it.

Serves 10–12

INGREDIENTS
115 g/4 oz/½ cup butter, softened
few drops of vanilla essence
115 g/4 oz/½ cup caster sugar
2 eggs
115 g/4 oz/1 cup self-raising flour,
   sifted
60 ml/4 tbsp milk
25 g/1 oz/⅓ cup desiccated coconut,
   to decorate
fresh rosebuds, or other flowers,
   to decorate

FOR THE LIGHT CHOCOLATE FILLING
115 g/4 oz/½ cup butter, softened
30 ml/2 tbsp icing sugar, sifted
75 g/3 oz plain chocolate, melted
250 ml/8 fl oz/1 cup double cream,
   lightly whipped

FOR THE DARK CHOCOLATE FILLING
115 g/4 oz plain chocolate,
   chopped
115 g/4 oz/½ cup butter
2 eggs
30 ml/2 tbsp caster sugar
250 ml/8 fl oz/1 cup double cream,
   lightly whipped
50 g/2 oz/½ cup cocoa powder
15 ml/1 tbsp dark rum
30 ml/2 tbsp powdered gelatine
   dissolved in 30 ml/2 tbsp
   hot water

FOR THE WHITE CHOCOLATE TOPPING
225 g/8 oz white chocolate
115 g/4 oz/½ cup butter

flowers
vanilla essence
powdered gelatine
eggs
rum
cream
icing sugar
plain chocolate
cocoa powder
dessicated coconut
caster sugar
butter
white chocolate
milk
self-raising flour

1 Preheat the oven to 180°C/350°F/Gas 4. Grease a 900 g/2 lb loaf tin, line the base and sides with greaseproof paper and grease the paper.

2 To make the cake, place the butter, vanilla essence and sugar in a mixing bowl and beat until light and fluffy. Add the eggs, one at a time, beating well after each addition. Sift the flour again and fold it and the milk into the cake mixture.

3 Transfer the cake mixture to the prepared tin and bake in the centre of the oven for 25–30 minutes or until a skewer inserted into the centre of the cake comes out clean. Leave the cake in the tin for about 5 minutes, then turn out on to a wire rack, peel off the lining paper and leave to cool completely.

4 To make the light chocolate filling, place the butter and icing sugar in a mixing bowl and beat until creamy. Add the chocolate and cream and mix until evenly blended. Cover and set aside in the fridge, until required.

5 To make the dark chocolate filling, place the chocolate and butter in a small saucepan and heat very gently, stirring frequently, until melted. Set aside to cool. Place the eggs and sugar in a bowl and beat with an electric mixer until thick and frothy. Gently fold in the cooled chocolate mixture, cream, cocoa, rum and dissolved gelatine until thoroughly blended.

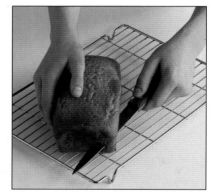

6 Wash and dry the loaf tin, then line with clear film, allowing plenty of film to hang over the edges. Using a long serrated knife, cut the cake horizontally into three layers.

7 Make the white chocolate topping. Melt the chocolate and butter in a small saucepan over a very gentle heat, stirring frequently. Cool slightly.

8 Spread two of the cake layers with the light chocolate filling, then place one of these layers, filling side up, in the base of the tin. Cover with half of the dark chocolate filling; chill for 10 minutes. Place the second light chocolate-topped layer in the terrine, filling side up. Spread over the remaining dark chocolate filling; chill for 10 minutes. Top with the remaining cake layer and chill the terrine in the fridge as before.

9 Turn the terrine out on to a wire rack, removing the clear film. Trim the edges, then pour over the white chocolate topping, spreading it evenly over the sides. Sprinkle the coconut over the top and sides. When set, transfer to a serving plate and decorate with fresh rosebuds or other flowers.

Bûche de Noël

This is the traditional French Christmas cake, filled with a chestnut purée and coated with a classic chocolate ganache.

Serves 8

INGREDIENTS
4 eggs
115 g/4 oz/½ cup caster sugar
75 g/3 oz/¾ cup plain flour
25 g/1 oz/¼ cup cocoa powder
icing sugar, crumbled chocolate
    flakes and holly leaves,
    to decorate

FOR THE MERINGUE MUSHROOMS
1 egg white
50 g/2 oz/¼ cup caster sugar, plus
    extra for sprinkling

FOR THE FILLING AND ICING
225 g/8 oz/scant 1 cup unsweetened
    chestnut purée
30 ml/2 tbsp clear honey
30 ml/2 tbsp brandy
300 ml/½ pint/1¼ cups
    double cream
150 g/5 oz/scant 1 cup plain
    chocolate chips

eggs

clear honey

cream

chocolate chips

brandy

cocoa powder

caster sugar

icing sugar

plain flour

chestnut purée

1 Preheat the oven to 200°C/400°F/ Gas 6. Line and grease a 30 x 20 cm/ 12 x 8 in Swiss roll tin. Whisk the eggs and sugar in a heatproof bowl over barely simmering water until thick and pale. Remove from the heat and continue to whisk until the mixture is cool and the beaters leave a thick trail on the surface. Mix the flour and cocoa powder; sift over the mixture and fold in gently. Spoon into the tin, level and bake for 12–15 minutes until the cake springs back when lightly pressed.

2 Place a sheet of non-stick baking paper on a lightly dampened dish towel and sprinkle liberally with caster sugar. Turn the cake over on the paper and leave to cool completely with the tin in place. Reduce the oven temperature to 110°C/225°F/Gas ¼.

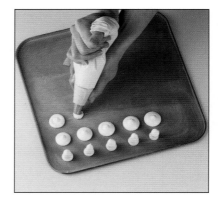

3 Make the meringue mushrooms. Whisk the egg white until stiff and gradually beat in the sugar, until thick and glossy. Transfer to a piping bag fitted with a plain nozzle. Pipe eight tall 'stalks' and eight shorter 'caps' on to a greased and floured baking sheet. Bake for 2½–3 hours, until crisp and dried out. Remove from the oven and leave to cool completely.

4 Make the filling. Blend the chestnut purée with the honey and brandy in a food processor until smooth, and gradually blend in half the cream until thick. Chill until required.

5 Make the icing. Melt the chocolate chips and remaining cream in a small pan over a low heat. Transfer to a bowl, cool and chill for 1 hour. Beat until thick.

6 Lift off the Swiss roll tin and peel away the lining paper from the sponge. Spread with all but 30 ml/2 tbsp of the chestnut filling, leaving a clear border. Roll up from one narrow end. Transfer to a cake board.

7 Coat the top and sides of the roll with the icing, leaving the ends plain. Swirl a pattern over the icing with a palette knife to resemble tree bark. Sprinkle the crumbled chocolate flakes over the rest of the board.

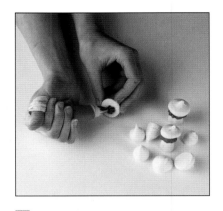

8 Remove the meringue 'stalks' and 'caps' from the baking sheet. Transfer the reserved chestnut filling to a piping bag, fitted with a star nozzle. Pipe a swirl on to the underside of each mushroom 'cap'. Press gently on to the 'stalks' to form the mushroom decorations.

9 Place a small cluster of mushrooms on top of the chocolate log, arranging the rest around the board. Sprinkle over a little icing sugar and add a few festive holly leaves if you like.

COOK'S TIP
The chocolate log will keep for up to two days in the fridge, in an airtight container. Do not assemble the mushrooms until just before serving, or they will soften.

Glazed Christmas Ring

A good, rich fruit cake is a must at Christmas. This one is particularly festive with its vibrant, glazed fruit-and-nut topping.

Serves 16–20

INGREDIENTS

225 g/8 oz/1⅓ cups sultanas
175 g/6 oz/1 cup raisins
175 g/6 oz/1 cup currants
175 g/6 oz/1 cup dried figs, chopped
90 ml/6 tbsp whisky
45 ml/3 tbsp orange juice
225 g/8 oz/1 cup butter
225 g/8 oz/1 cup soft dark brown sugar
5 eggs
250 g/9 oz/2¼ cups plain flour
15 ml/1 tbsp baking powder
15 ml/1 tbsp ground mixed spice
150 g/5 oz/⅔ cup glacé cherries, chopped
115 g/4 oz/1 cup brazil nuts, chopped
50 g/2 oz/⅓ cup chopped mixed candied peel
50 g/2 oz/⅓ cup ground almonds
grated rind and juice of 1 orange
30 ml/2 tbsp thick-cut orange marmalade

TO DECORATE

275 g/10 oz/1 cup thick-cut orange marmalade
15 ml/1 tbsp orange juice
175 g/6 oz/¾ cup mixed colour glacé cherries
175 g/6 oz/1½ cups whole brazil nuts
115 g/4 oz/⅔ cup dried figs, halved

1 Place the sultanas, raisins, currants and figs in a large bowl. Pour over 60 ml/4 tbsp of the whisky and the orange juice and leave to macerate overnight.

4 Sift the remaining flour, baking powder and mixed spice together. Fold into the creamed mixture. Add the remaining ingredients, reserving the whisky, then stir in the macerated fruit. Transfer the mixture to the tin, smooth the surface and make a small dip in the centre. Bake for 1 hour, reduce the oven temperature to 150°C/300°F/Gas 2 and bake for a further 1¾–2 hours.

2 Preheat the oven to 160°C/325°F/Gas 3. Grease and double line a 25 cm/10 in ring or tube tin.

5 Test the cake with a skewer to ensure it is cooked, then remove it from the oven. Prick the cake all over with a skewer and pour over the reserved whisky. Leave to cool in the tin for 30 minutes, then transfer to a wire rack to cool completely.

3 Cream the butter and sugar together until pale and light. Beat in the eggs one at a time, beating well after each addition, until incorporated. Add a little flour if the mixture starts to curdle.

6 To decorate, heat the marmalade and orange juice together in a pan and boil gently for 3 minutes. Stir in the cherries, nuts and figs. Remove from the heat and cool slightly.

7 Spoon the glazed fruits and nuts over the cake in an attractive pattern and leave to set.

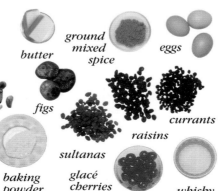

butter

ground mixed spice

eggs

figs

currants

raisins

orange

brazil nuts

ground almonds

plain flour

mixed candied peel

baking powder

sultanas

glacé cherries

whisky

soft dark brown sugar

Fruit-and-Nut Cake

A rich fruit cake that improves with keeping.

Serves 12–14

INGREDIENTS

175 g/6 oz/1½ cups self-raising
   wholemeal flour
175 g/6 oz/1½ cups self-raising
   white flour
10 ml/2 tsp ground mixed spice
15 ml/1 tbsp apple and apricot
   spread
45 ml/3 tbsp clear honey
15 ml/1 tbsp molasses or black
   treacle
90 ml/6 tbsp sunflower oil
175 ml/6 fl oz/¾ cup orange juice
2 eggs, beaten
675 g/1½ lb/4 cups luxury mixed
   dried fruit
45 ml/3 tbsp split almonds
115 g/4 oz/½ cup glacé
   cherries, halved

molasses

*luxury mixed
dried fruit*

*clear
honey*

*ground
mixed spice*

eggs

*apple and
apricot spread*

*orange
juice*

*split
almonds*

*sunflower
oil*

*self-raising
white flour*

*glacé
cherries*

*self-raising
wholemeal flour*

1 Preheat the oven to 160°C/325°F/
Gas 3. Grease and line a deep round
20 cm/8 in cake tin. Secure a band of
brown paper around the outside.

2 Sift the flours into a mixing bowl
with the mixed spice and make a well in
the centre.

COOK'S TIP

For a less elaborate cake, omit the
cherries, chop the almonds roughly
and sprinkle them over the top.

3 Put the apple and apricot spread in a
small bowl. Gradually stir in the honey
and molasses or treacle. Add to the dry
ingredients with the oil, orange juice,
eggs and mixed fruit. Mix thoroughly.

4 Turn the mixture into the prepared
tin and smooth the surface. Arrange the
almonds and cherries in a pattern over
the top. Stand the tin on newspaper and
bake for 2 hours or until a skewer
inserted into the centre comes out clean.
Transfer to a wire rack until cold, then lift
out of the tin and remove the paper.

Panettone

This famous fruit cake comes from Italy, where it is often served with a glass of red wine.

Makes 1 cake

INGREDIENTS

150 ml/¼ pint/⅔ cup lukewarm milk
1 sachet dried yeast
350 g/12 oz/3 cups flour
75 g/3 oz/6 tbsp granulated sugar
10 ml/2 tsp salt
2 eggs, plus 5 egg yolks
175 g/6 oz/¾ cup butter, softened
115 g/4 oz/⅔ cup raisins
grated rind of 1 lemon
50 g/2 oz/½ cup chopped candied
    peel

milk

lemon rind

butter

salt

raisins

flour

egg yolks

granulated sugar

candied peel

dried yeast

eggs

1 Mix the milk and yeast in a large warmed bowl and leave for 10 minutes, until frothy. Stir in 115 g/4 oz/1 cup of the flour, cover loosely and leave in a warm place for 30 minutes. Sift over the remaining flour. Make a well in the centre and add the sugar, salt, eggs and egg yolks.

2 Stir with a spoon, then with your hands, to obtain a soft, sticky dough.

3 Smear over the butter, then work it in. Cover and leave to rise in a warm place for 3–4 hours, until the dough has doubled in bulk.

4 Line the bottom of a 2 litre/3½ pint/8¾ cup charlotte tin with non-stick baking paper, then grease well. Knock down the dough and transfer to a floured surface. Knead in the raisins, lemon rind and candied peel. Shape the dough and fit it into the tin.

5 Cover the tin with a plastic bag and leave to rise for about 2 hours until the dough is well above the top of the tin.

6 Preheat the oven to 200°C/400°F/Gas 6. Bake for 15 minutes, cover the top with foil and lower the heat to 180°C/350°F/Gas 4. Bake for 30 minutes more. Allow to cool in the tin for about 5 minutes, then transfer to a rack.

COOK'S TIP

If you do not have a charlotte tin, you can use a perfectly clean 1 kg/2¼ lb coffee or fruit can.

Simnel Cake

This traditional Easter cake has a layer of marzipan in the centre.

Serves 10

INGREDIENTS
450 g/1 lb marzipan
225 g/8 oz/1⅓ cups raisins
175 g/6 oz/1 cup sultanas
50 g/2 oz/⅓ cup glacé cherries, quartered
50 g/2 oz/½ cup mixed candied peel
175 g/6 oz/¾ cup butter, softened
175 g/6 oz/¾ cup caster sugar
4 eggs
225 g/8 oz/2 cups plain flour
5 ml/1 tsp baking powder
5 ml/1 tsp ground mixed spice
30 ml/2 tbsp apricot glaze
175 g/6 oz/1½ cups icing sugar, sifted
marzipan flowers, to decorate

glacé cherries

icing sugar

eggs

marzipan

butter

ground mixed spice

mixed candied peel

baking powder

caster sugar

flour

raisins

apricot glaze

sultanas

1 Roll out half the marzipan thinly on a surface lightly dusted with icing sugar. Using the base of an 18 cm/7 in round deep cake tin, cut out a marzipan round.

2 Grease and double line the tin and preheat the oven to 160°C/325°F/Gas 3. Mix the raisins, sultanas, glacé cherries and mixed candied peel.

3 Beat the butter with the sugar in a bowl, until light and fluffy. Separate one egg and set the white and yolk aside. Add the remaining eggs to the cake mixture, one at a time, beating well after each addition. Sift the flour, baking powder and mixed spice into the bowl; fold in gently. Add the mixed fruit and fold in evenly.

COOK'S TIP

To make apricot glaze, heat 225 g/8 oz/⅔ cup apricot jam in a pan until melted, then press through a strainer into a clean pan. Bring to the boil, then cool slightly.

4 Place half of the mixture in the tin and level. Place the marzipan round on top, pressing down to level. Spoon the remaining cake mixture on top, smooth the top and make a slight depression in the centre. Bake for 2¼–2½ hours until the cake is golden brown. Test with a skewer. Cool in the tin, then turn the cake out, remove the paper and place on a wire rack.

5 Roll out two-thirds of the remaining marzipan, and cut an 18 cm/7 in circle. Brush the top of the cake with apricot glaze and cover with the marzipan round.

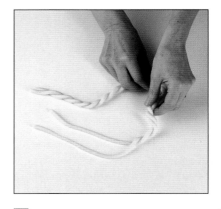

6 Shape the remaining marzipan into 11 eggs and a rope for the rim of the cake; secure with apricot glaze. Put the cake on a baking sheet.

7 Preheat the grill. Brush all the marzipan with egg yolk and grill quickly until tinged with golden brown. Leave until cold.

8 Beat the egg white and icing sugar until thick and glossy. Spread the icing in the centre of the cake. When set, decorate with marzipan flowers. Add ribbons, if you like.

Strawberry Chocolate Valentine Gâteau

Offering a slice of this voluptuous Valentine gâteau could be the start of a very special romance.

Serves 8

INGREDIENTS
175 g/6 oz/1½ cups self-raising flour
10 ml/2 tsp baking powder
75 ml/5 tbsp cocoa powder
115 g/4 oz/½ cup caster sugar
2 eggs, beaten
15 ml/1 tbsp black treacle
150 ml/¼ pint/⅔ cup sunflower oil
150 ml/¼ pint/⅔ cup milk

FOR THE FILLING
45 ml/3 tbsp strawberry jam
150 ml/¼ pint/⅔ cup double or
    whipping cream, whipped
115 g/4 oz strawberries, sliced

TO DECORATE
chocolate covering fondant
chocolate hearts
icing sugar

caster sugar   *cocoa powder*   *cream*

black treacle   *sunflower oil*   *baking powder*

icing sugar   *self-raising flour*   *strawberries*   *strawberry jam*   *milk*   *eggs*

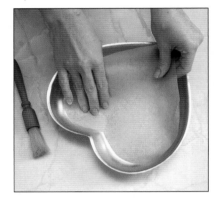

1 Preheat the oven to 160°C/325°F/ Gas 3. Grease a deep 20 cm/8 in heart-shaped cake tin and line the base with non-stick baking paper. Sift the flour, baking powder and cocoa into a mixing bowl. Stir in the sugar, then make a well in the centre.

2 Add the eggs, treacle, oil and milk. Mix quickly with a spoon, then beat with a hand-held electric mixer until smooth and creamy.

3 Spoon the mixture into the prepared cake tin and spread evenly. Bake for about 45 minutes, until well risen and firm to the touch. Cool in the tin for a few minutes, then turn out on to a wire rack to cool completely.

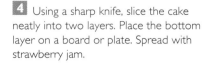

4 Using a sharp knife, slice the cake neatly into two layers. Place the bottom layer on a board or plate. Spread with strawberry jam.

5 Sandwich the cake layers together with the strawberries and cream, cover the cake with the fondant and decorate with hearts. Dust with icing sugar.

Double Heart Engagement Cake

For a celebratory engagement party, these sumptuous cakes make the perfect centrepiece.

Serves 20

INGREDIENTS
225 g/8 oz/1 cup soft margarine
225 g/8 oz/1 cup caster sugar
225 g/8 oz/2 cups self-raising flour, sifted
10 ml/2 tsp baking powder
4 eggs
30 ml/2 tbsp cocoa powder mixed with 30 ml/2 tbsp boiling water

FOR THE BUTTERCREAM
225 g/8 oz/1 cup butter, softened
450 g/1 lb/4 cups icing sugar, sifted
15 ml/1 tbsp bottled coffee essence

FOR THE DECORATION
350 g/12 oz plain chocolate
icing sugar
fresh raspberries

eggs

plain chocolate

icing sugar

raspberries

margarine

self-raising flour

caster sugar

cocoa powder

baking powder

coffee essence

butter

1 Preheat the oven to 160°C/325°F/Gas 3. Grease and base-line two 20 cm/8 in heart-shaped cake tins. Mix all the cake ingredients in a bowl, using a wooden spoon, then beat for 1–2 minutes until smooth and glossy. Divide between the tins and smooth the surface. Bake for 25–30 minutes or until firm to the touch. Turn out on to wire racks, peel off the lining paper and leave to cool completely.

2 Meanwhile, melt the chocolate in a heatproof bowl over hot water. Pour on to a firm, smooth surface and spread the melted chocolate out evenly with a large palette knife. Leave the chocolate to cool slightly. It should feel just set, but not hard.

3 Make chocolate curls. Hold a large sharp knife at a 45° angle to the chocolate and draw it along the chocolate in short sawing movements. Leave the curls to firm on baking paper.

4 Cut each cake in half horizontally. Make the buttercream by beating the butter until fluffy, then stirring in the icing sugar and coffee essence. Use about one-third of the mixture to sandwich both cakes together. Use the remaining icing to cover the cakes.

5 Place the cakes on cake boards. Generously cover the tops and sides of both cakes with the chocolate curls, pressing them gently into the buttercream. Dust with icing sugar and decorate with raspberries. Chill until ready to serve.

White Chocolate Celebration Cake

Every occasion is a special celebration when you serve a superb cake like this one.

Serves 40–50

INGREDIENTS
900 g/2 lb/8 cups plain flour
2.5 ml/½ tsp salt
20 ml/4 tsp bicarbonate of soda
450 g/1 lb white chocolate, chopped
475 ml/16 fl oz/2 cups whipping cream
450 g/1 lb/2 cups butter, softened
900 g/2 lb/4 cups caster sugar
12 eggs
20 ml/4 tsp lemon essence
grated rind of 2 lemons
600 ml/1 pint/2½ cups buttermilk
lemon curd, for filling
chocolate leaves, to decorate

FOR THE LEMON SYRUP
250 g/9 oz/1 cup granulated sugar
250 ml/8 fl oz/1 cup water
60 ml/4 tbsp lemon juice

FOR THE BUTTERCREAM
675 g/1½ lb white chocolate
1 kg/2¼ lb/4½ cups cream cheese,
500 g/1¼ lb/2½ cups butter, softened
60 ml/4 tbsp lemon juice
5 ml/1 tsp lemon essence

1 Divide all the ingredients into two equal batches, so that the quantities are more manageable. Use each batch to make one cake. Preheat the oven to 180°C/350°F/Gas 4. Grease a 30 cm/12 in round cake tin. Base-line with non-stick baking paper. Sift the flour, salt and bicarbonate of soda into a bowl and set aside. Melt the chocolate and cream in a saucepan over a low heat, stirring until smooth. Set aside to cool.

2 Cream the butter with the sugar in a bowl. Beat in the eggs, then the melted chocolate and cream, the lemon essence and rind. Gradually add the flour mixture, alternately with the buttermilk. Pour into the tin and bake for 1 hour or until a skewer inserted in the cake comes out clean. Cool in the tin for 10 minutes, then turn out on a wire rack and cool completely. Using the second batch of ingredients, make another cake in the same way.

3 Make the lemon syrup. Heat the sugar and water in a small saucepan, stirring until the sugar dissolves. Bring to the boil. Stir in the lemon juice and cool, covered with clear film.

4 Make the buttercream. Melt the white chocolate in a heatproof bowl over hot water. Beat the cream cheese until smooth. Gradually beat in the chocolate, then the butter, lemon juice and essence. Split each cake in half to make two equal layers. Spoon syrup over each layer, let it soak in, then repeat. Sandwich the layers together with lemon curd.

eggs
white chocolate
chocolate leaves
lemon
caster sugar
butter
buttermilk
flour
cream
bicarbonate of soda
salt
granulated sugar
water
lemon juice
cream cheese

5 Spread a quarter of the buttercream over the top of one filled cake. Place the second filled cake on top. Put the cake on a serving plate. Set aside a quarter of the buttercream for piping, then spread the rest over the cake.

6 Spoon the reserved buttercream into a large icing bag fitted with a small star tip. Pipe a shell pattern around the cake. Decorate with chocolate leaves. Add fresh flowers, if you like.

Mocha-hazelnut Battenberg

The traditional Battenberg cake originated in Germany when the Prince of Battenberg married Queen Victoria's daughter, Beatrice. This recipe is a variation on the original theme.

Serves 6–8

INGREDIENTS
115 g/4 oz/½ cup butter, softened
115 g/4 oz/½ cup caster sugar
2 eggs
115 g/4 oz/1 cup self-raising flour, sifted
50 g/2 oz/½ cup ground hazelnuts
10 ml/2 tsp coffee essence
15 ml/1 tbsp cocoa powder

TO FINISH
105 ml/7 tbsp apricot jam, warmed and sieved
225 g/8 oz yellow marzipan
115 g/4 oz/1 cup ground hazelnuts
sifted icing sugar

coffee essence

icing sugar

eggs

butter

caster sugar

ground hazelnuts

self-raising flour

apricot jam

cocoa powder

marzipan

1 Preheat the oven to 180°C/350°F/ Gas 4. Grease an 18 cm/7 in square cake tin, line the base with greaseproof paper and grease the paper.

2 Place the butter and sugar in a bowl and beat until fluffy. Gradually beat in the eggs, then fold in the flour. Transfer half the mixture to another bowl.

3 Stir the ground hazelnuts into one half of the cake mixture and the coffee essence and cocoa powder into the other half.

4 Prepare a strip of foil to fit the width and height of the cake tin, then place the mocha-flavoured cake mixture in one half of the tin. Position the strip of foil down the centre, then spoon the hazelnut-flavoured cake mixture into the other half of the tin. Smooth the surface of both mixtures.

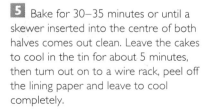

5 Bake for 30–35 minutes or until a skewer inserted into the centre of both halves comes out clean. Leave the cakes to cool in the tin for about 5 minutes, then turn out on to a wire rack, peel off the lining paper and leave to cool completely.

6 Separate the cakes and cut each one in half lengthways. Take one portion of the mocha-flavoured cake and brush along one side with a little apricot jam. Sandwich this surface with a portion of the hazelnut-flavoured cake. Brush the top of the cakes with apricot jam and position the other portion of mocha-flavoured cake on top of the hazelnut base. Brush along the inner long side with apricot jam and sandwich with the final portion of hazelnut-flavoured cake. Set aside.

7 Knead the marzipan on a work surface to soften, then knead in half the ground hazelnuts until evenly blended. Dust the work surface lightly with icing sugar and roll out the marzipan into a rectangle large enough to wrap around the cake, excluding the ends.

8 Brush the long sides of the cake with apricot jam, then lay the cake on top of the marzipan. Wrap the marzipan around the cake, sealing the edge neatly. Place the cake on a serving plate, seal-side down, and pinch the edges of the marzipan to give an attractive finish. Score the top surface with a knife and sprinkle with the remaining ground hazelnuts.

Mocha Brazil Layer Torte

This wonderfully rich gâteau marries meringue and sponge layers with a mocha icing.

Serves 12

INGREDIENTS
4 eggs, plus 3 egg whites
225 g/8 oz/1 cup caster sugar
45 ml/3 tbsp coffee essence
75 g/3 oz/¾ cup brazil nuts, toasted
    and finely ground
275 g/10 oz/1¾ cups plain chocolate
    chips
115 g/4 oz/1 cup plain flour
5 ml/1 tsp baking powder
30 ml/2 tbsp water
600 ml/1 pint/2½ cups double
    cream

To DECORATE
50 g/2 oz plain chocolate
12 chocolate-coated coffee beans

plain
chocolate
chips

brazil
nuts

double cream

chocolate-
coated
coffee beans

plain
flour

eggs

baking
powder

caster sugar

plain
chocolate

coffee
essence

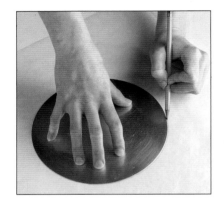

1 Preheat the oven to 150°C/300°F/ Gas 2. Draw two 20 cm/8 in circles on non-stick baking paper. Place on a baking sheet. Grease, base-line and flour a 20 cm/8 in round springform tin.

3 Bake for 1¾–2 hours, until crisp and golden. Remove from the oven and transfer to a wire rack to cool completely. Peel away the baking paper. Increase the oven temperature to 180°C/350°F/Gas 4.

2 Whisk the 3 egg whites until stiff and gradually whisk in half the sugar, 30 ml/2 tbsp at a time, until thick and glossy. Fold in 15 ml/1 tbsp of the coffee essence and all the nuts until evenly incorporated. Transfer to a piping bag fitted with a plain nozzle. Starting in the centre, pipe circles of mixture on to the prepared paper.

4 To prepare the chocolate decorations, melt the chocolate. Pour over a sheet of non-stick baking paper, spread out to a very thin layer with a palette knife and leave to set.

5 Melt 115 g/4 oz/¾ cup of the chocolate chips and cool slightly. Whisk the 4 whole eggs and remaining sugar in a bowl over simmering water, until pale and thick. Remove from the heat, continue beating until cool and carefully stir in the melted chocolate. Sift the flour and baking powder together and fold into the whisked mixture. Transfer to the prepared tin and bake for 40–45 minutes, until risen and springy to the touch. Cool in the tin for 10 minutes, then transfer to a wire rack to cool completely.

6 To make the icing, melt the remaining chocolate chips and coffee essence with the water in a bowl over hot water, then cool slightly. Whip the cream until it holds its shape; stir into the mocha mixture.

 Cut the cooled cake into three equal layers. Trim the meringue discs to the same size and assemble the gâteau with alternate layers of sponge, icing and meringue, finishing with sponge. Reserve a little of the remaining icing for decoration; use the rest to coat the cake.

8 Peel away the paper from the set chocolate and cut out 12 triangles.

9 Use the reserved icing to pipe 24 small rosettes around the rim of the cake. Decorate with the coffee beans and chocolate triangles.

Hazelnut Praline and Apricot Genoese

A simple whisked sponge tastes spectacular layered with apricot and maple icing.

Serves 12

INGREDIENTS

4 eggs
115 g/4 oz/½ cup caster sugar
75 g/3 oz/6 tbsp melted butter,
   slightly cooled
50 g/2 oz/½ cup plain flour, sifted
25 g/1 oz/⅓ cup toasted ground
   hazelnuts

FOR THE PRALINE
75 g/3 oz/6 tbsp granulated sugar
75 g/3 oz/¾ cup shelled hazelnuts

FOR THE ICING AND DECORATION
6 egg yolks
175 g/6 oz/¾ cup caster sugar
150 ml/¼ pint/⅔ cup milk
350 g/12 oz/1½ cups butter, diced
30 ml/2 tbsp golden syrup
400 g/14 oz can apricot halves in
   natural juice

1 Make the praline. Heat the sugar and nuts together in a small heavy-based pan, until the sugar melts. Increase the heat, and stir until the sugar turns golden. Do not let it burn. Remove immediately from the heat. Carefully scoop out 12 coated nuts and place on an oiled baking sheet. Pour the remaining mixture on to a separate area of the sheet and leave until set. Break into pieces and grind in a food processor to form a rough paste.

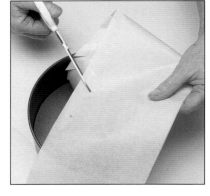

2 Preheat the oven to 180°C/350°F/ Gas 4. Grease, line and flour a 23 cm/ 9 in springform tin. Whisk the eggs and sugar in a heatproof bowl over simmering water until thick and pale. Remove from the heat and continue whisking until cool. Fold in the butter, flour and ground hazelnuts. Transfer to the prepared tin. Bake for 35 minutes until risen and springy to the touch. Cool in the tin for 10 minutes, then transfer to a wire rack to cool completely.

3 Make the icing. Beat the egg yolks and caster sugar until pale and thick. Bring the milk to the boil and pour over the creamed mixture, still beating. Return to the pan and stir over a low heat, until the mixture coats the back of the spoon. Strain into a large bowl. Beat the mixture until tepid. Gradually beat in the butter, a little at a time, until the mixture is thick and glossy. Beat in the golden syrup, then beat in 15 ml/1 tbsp of the juice from the canned apricots.

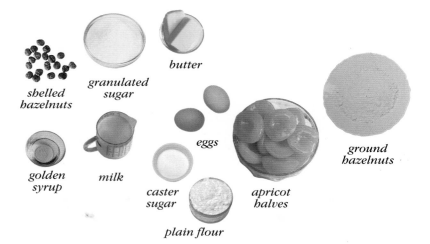

shelled hazelnuts *granulated sugar* *butter* *golden syrup* *milk* *eggs* *caster sugar* *plain flour* *apricot halves* *ground hazelnuts*

COOK'S TIP
Grind nuts with a nut mill, clean coffee grinder or a food processor. Use a small batch of nuts at a time to ensure an even texture.

4 Cut the cold cake into three layers. Reserve 4 apricot halves and chop the rest. Fold the chopped fruit into one-third of the icing with 45 ml/3 tbsp of the praline paste. Spread one layer of sponge with half the fruit filling, top with the next layer of sponge and repeat.

5 Reserve a little of the remaining icing for decoration. Use the rest to cover the top and sides of the cake. Coat the sides with the remaining praline paste and mark a pattern over the top with a palette knife. Using the reserved icing, pipe rosettes around the top of the cake, and decorate with slices of apricot and praline-coated nuts.

Walnut and Ricotta Cake

Soft, tangy ricotta cheese is widely used in Italian sweets. Here, it is included along with walnuts and orange to flavour a whisked egg sponge. Don't worry if it sinks slightly after baking – this gives it an authentic appearance.

Makes 10 slices

INGREDIENTS
115 g/4 oz/1 cup walnut pieces
150 g/5 oz/⅔ cup butter, softened
150 g/5 oz/⅔ cup caster sugar
5 eggs, separated
finely grated rind of 1 orange
150 g/5 oz/⅔ cup ricotta cheese
40 g/1½ oz/6 tbsp plain flour

TO FINISH
60 ml/4 tbsp apricot jam
15 ml/1 tbsp water
30 ml/2 tbsp brandy
50 g/2 oz plain chocolate, coarsely
    grated

brandy
butter
ricotta cheese
apricot jam
walnut pieces
orange rind
plain flour
plain chocolate
caster sugar
eggs

1 Preheat the oven to 190°C/375° F/ Gas 5. Grease and line the base of a deep 23 cm/9 in round, loose-based cake tin. Roughly chop the walnuts and toast them lightly.

2 Cream the butter and 115g/4 oz/ ½ cup of the sugar until light and fluffy. Add the egg yolks, orange rind, ricotta cheese, flour and walnuts and mix well.

COOK'S TIP
Use toasted and chopped almonds in place of the walnuts.

3 Whisk the egg whites until stiff. Gradually whisk in the remaining sugar. Fold a quarter of the whisked whites into the ricotta mixture. Carefully fold in the rest. Turn the mixture into the prepared tin. Bake for about 30 minutes until risen and firm. Leave to cool in the tin.

4 Transfer the cake to a serving plate. Heat the apricot jam with the water in a small saucepan. Press through a sieve into a bowl; stir in the brandy. Brush over the top and sides of the cake. Scatter the cake generously with the grated chocolate.

Baked Cheesecake with Fresh Fruits

Exotic fruits contrast with the creaminess of this light and luscious cheesecake.

Serves 12

INGREDIENTS
175 g/6 oz/1⅓ cups digestive
   biscuits, crushed
50 g/2 oz/¼ cup butter, melted
450 g/1 lb/1 cup full-fat soft cheese
150 ml/¼ pint/⅔ cup soured cream
115 g/4 oz/½ cup caster sugar
3 eggs, separated
grated rind of 1 lemon
30 ml/2 tbsp Marsala
2.5 ml/½ tsp almond essence
50 g/2 oz/⅓ cup sultanas
450 g/1 lb prepared mixed fruits,
   to decorate

digestive biscuits

full-fat soft cheese

butter

sultanas

almond essence

caster sugar

grated lemon rind

eggs

mixed fruits

soured cream

Marsala

lemon

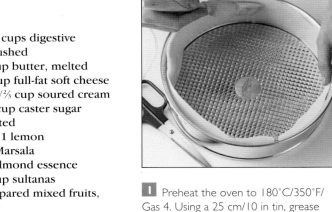

1 Preheat the oven to 180°C/350°F/ Gas 4. Using a 25 cm/10 in tin, grease and line the sides.

2 Combine the biscuits with the butter until well combined and press on to the bottom of the prepared tin. Smooth the surface with a metal spoon and chill for 20 minutes.

4 Whisk the egg whites until stiff and fold into the creamed mixture with the sultanas until evenly combined. Pour over the chilled biscuit base and bake for 45 minutes, until risen and just set in the centre.

5 Remove from the oven and leave in the tin in a warm, draught-free place, until completely cold. Carefully remove the tin and peel away the lining paper. Chill the cheesecake for at least an hour. Decorate with the prepared fruits just before serving.

3 Meanwhile prepare the cake mixture. Beat the cheese, cream, sugar, egg yolks, lemon rind, Marsala and almond essence together until smooth and creamy.

Strawberry Shortcake

This is a cross between a shortbread and a cake, resulting in a light biscuit-textured sponge. It is quick and easy to prepare.

Serves 8

INGREDIENTS
225 g/8 oz fresh strawberries, hulled
30 ml/2 tbsp ruby port
225 g/8 oz/2 cups self-raising flour
10 ml/2 tsp baking powder
75 g/3 oz/6 tbsp butter, diced, plus a
    little melted butter, to glaze
40 g/1½ oz/3 tbsp caster sugar
1 egg, lightly beaten
15–30 ml/1–2 tbsp milk
250 ml/8 fl oz/1 cup double cream
icing sugar, for dusting

double cream   butter

icing sugar

ruby port

egg   caster sugar   milk

baking powder   self-raising flour

strawberries

1 Preheat the oven to 220°C/425°F/ Gas 7. Grease and base-line two 20 cm/ 8 in round, loose-based cake tins. Reserve five strawberries for decoration. Cut the rest into slices and marinate in the port for 1–2 hours.

2 Sift the flour and baking powder into a bowl. Rub in the butter until the mixture resembles fine breadcrumbs. Stir in the sugar. Work in the egg and 15 ml/1 tbsp of the milk to form a soft dough, adding more milk if the dough is too firm.

3 Knead the dough on a lightly floured surface and divide in two. Roll out each half, mark one half into eight wedges, and transfer to the prepared tins. Brush each with a little melted butter and bake for 15 minutes until risen and golden. Remove from the oven, cool in the tins for 10 minutes, then transfer to a wire rack to cool completely.

4 Strain the macerated strawberries, reserving the port. Cut the marked cake into wedges. Whip the cream until it holds its shape, then set aside a little for decoration. Fold the reserved port and strawberry slices into the whipped cream and spread over the whole shortcake.

5 Arrange the wedges, overlapping slightly, on top of the filling. Spoon the reserved cream into a piping bag fitted with a star nozzle and pipe a swirl on each wedge. Cut four of the reserved strawberries in half, and use to decorate each swirl. Slit the final strawberry and place it in the centre of the cake. Dust with icing sugar.

Iced Paradise Cake

Home-made sponge fingers and a rich mixture of chocolate and rum make an iced gâteau that is aptly named.

Serves 12

INGREDIENTS

3 eggs
75 g/3 oz/6 tbsp caster sugar
65 g/2½ oz/10 tbsp plain flour
15 g/½ oz/2 tbsp cornflour
90 ml/6 tbsp dark rum
250 g/9 oz/1⅓ cups plain chocolate
    chips
30 ml/2 tbsp golden syrup
30 ml/2 tbsp water
400 ml/14 fl oz/1⅔ cups double
    cream
115 g/4 oz/1⅓ cups desiccated
    coconut, toasted
25 g/1 oz/2 tbsp butter, diced
30 ml/2 tbsp single cream

To decorate

25–50 g/1–2 oz/⅓ cup white
    chocolate chips
a little desiccated coconut or
    coconut curls
a little cocoa powder

golden syrup   butter   dark rum   cocoa powder
chocolate chips   desiccated coconut   caster sugar
double cream
cornflour   eggs
plain flour

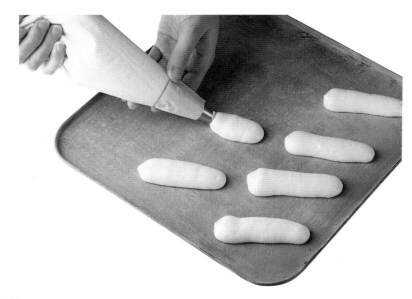

1 Preheat the oven to 200°C/400°F/ Gas 6. Grease and flour 2 large baking sheets. Line a 900 g/2 lb loaf tin with clear film. Whisk the eggs and sugar in a heatproof bowl over just simmering water until thick and pale. Remove from the heat and continue whisking until cool. Sift over the flour and cornflour and fold in.

2 Transfer the whisked sponge cake mixture to a piping bag and pipe about thirty 7.5 cm/3 in fingers on the prepared sheets. Bake for 8–10 minutes until risen and springy to the touch. Remove from the oven, cool slightly and transfer the sponge fingers to a wire rack to cool completely.

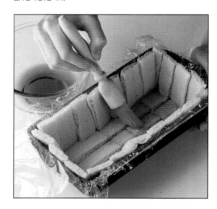

3 Line the base and sides of the prepared loaf tin with sponge fingers, trimming them as necessary to fit the tin. Brush with a little rum. Put 75 g/3 oz/ ½ cup of the plain chocolate chips in a heatproof bowl. Add the syrup, water and 30 ml/2 tbsp of the remaining rum. Place over a pan of simmering water, until the chocolate melts. Cool slightly.

4 Whip the double cream and stir in the chocolate mixture and toasted coconut. Pour into the tin, tap the bottom gently to clear any air bubbles, and place the remaining sponge fingers over the top. Brush over the remaining rum. Cover with clear film and freeze for several hours, until firm.

5 Melt the remaining plain chocolate chips and butter with the single cream over gently simmering water. Remove from the heat and cool the icing slightly. Remove the cake from the freezer; turn out on to a wire rack. Pour over the icing in one smooth motion, to coat the top and sides of the cake. Use a palette knife to smooth the sides, if necessary. Chill for 10–15 minutes, until the chocolate icing is set.

6 Melt the white chocolate chips and transfer to a greaseproof paper piping bag. Snip off the end and drizzle a zig-zag pattern over the chocolate icing. Allow the cake to soften until a knife will cut through easily. Just before serving, decorate with a little desiccated coconut or coconut curls, and dust lightly with cocoa powder.

Chestnut Cake

Rich, moist and heavy, this is definitely a cake to mark an occasion.

Serves 8–10

INGREDIENTS
225 g/8 oz/1 cup butter, softened
150 g/5 oz/⅔ cup caster sugar
439 g/15½ oz can chestnut purée
9 eggs, separated
150 g/5 oz/1¼ cups plain flour, sifted
pinch of salt
105 ml/7 tbsp dark rum
300 ml/½ pint/1¼ cups double cream

TO DECORATE
marrons glacés, chopped
icing sugar, sifted

chestnut purée

icing sugar

caster sugar

butter

eggs

double cream

dark rum

plain flour

COOK'S TIP
In order to have effective control over a piping bag, it is important to hold it in a relaxed position. Use one or both hands and keep up an even pressure.

1 Preheat the oven to 180°C/350°F/ Gas 4. Grease and base-line a 21 cm/ 8½ in springform cake tin. Cream the butter with three-quarters of the sugar in a bowl. Fold in two-thirds of the chestnut purée alternately with the egg yolks. Beat well. Fold in the flour and salt.

2 Whisk the egg whites in a clean, grease-free bowl until stiff. Beat a little of the egg whites into the chestnut mixture to lighten it, then fold in the remainder.

3 Transfer the cake mixture to the prepared tin and smooth the surface. Bake for 1¼ hours, or until a skewer inserted into the centre of the cake comes out clean. Place in the tin on a wire rack. Using a skewer, pierce holes evenly all over the cake. Sprinkle 60 ml/ 4 tbsp of the rum over the top, then allow the cake to cool completely before removing from the tin and peeling off the lining paper.

4 Cut the cake into two layers. Whisk the cream with the remaining rum, sugar and chestnut purée until thick. Sandwich the cake layers with two-thirds of the chestnut cream. Spread some of the remaining chestnut cream over the top and sides of the cake, then use the rest to pipe big swirls around the rim. Decorate with the marrons glacés. Dredge with sifted icing sugar.

Coffee, Peach and Almond Daquoise

This is a traditional meringue gâteau. The meringue mixture is piped into rounds, baked, and layered with a buttercream and peach filling.

Serves 12

INGREDIENTS
5 eggs, separated
400 g/14 oz/1¾ cups caster sugar
15 ml/1 tbsp cornflour
175 g/6 oz/1½ cups ground
    almonds, toasted
120 ml/4 fl oz/½ cup milk
275 g/10 oz/1¼ cups butter, diced
45–60 ml/3–4 tbsp coffee essence
2 x 400 g/14 oz cans peach halves in
    natural juice, drained
75 g/3 oz/1 cup flaked almonds,
    toasted
icing sugar, for dusting
mint leaves, to decorate

milk

eggs

cornflour

icing sugar

coffee essence

butter

flaked almonds

mint leaves

caster sugar

peach slices

ground almonds

1 Preheat the oven to 150°C/300°F/Gas 2. Draw three 23 cm/9 in circles on non-stick baking paper. Place on separate baking sheets. Whisk the egg whites until stiff. Gradually whisk in 275 g/10 oz/1¼ cups of the sugar, until thick and glossy. Fold in the cornflour and ground almonds. Pipe the mixture in a coil on each marked circle. Bake for about 2 hours until pale gold and dry. Cool on wire racks. Peel away the baking paper.

2 Make the custard icing. Beat the egg yolks and remaining caster sugar until pale and thick. Bring the milk to the boil and pour it over the creamed mixture, still beating. Return to the milk pan and stir over a low heat until the mixture coats the back of the spoon. Strain the custard into a large bowl.

3 Beat the custard until tepid. Beat in the butter gradually until the mixture is thick and glossy. Beat in the coffee essence. Reserve six peach slices for decoration; chop the rest and fold them into half the custard icing. Use this to sandwich the meringue discs together.

4 Use the remaining icing to coat the top and sides of the gâteau. Cover the top with the toasted almond flakes and dust liberally with icing sugar. Use the reserved peach slices with the mint leaves to decorate the rim of the gâteau. Serve as soon as possible.

Coconut Lime Layer Cake

Coconut is a deservedly popular cake ingredient. Here it also features as a crunchy topping on the meringue frosting.

Serves 8

INGREDIENTS
275 g/10 oz/2½ cups plain flour
12.5 ml/2½ tsp baking powder
1.5 ml/¼ tsp salt
150 g/5 oz/⅔ cup butter, softened
275 g/10 oz/1½ cups sugar
10 ml/2 tsp grated lime rind
3 eggs
120 ml/4 fl oz/½ cup fresh lime juice
120 ml/4 fl oz/½ cup water
60 g/2¼ oz/¾ cup dessicated
    coconut
American Frosting (see Basic Icings)

dessicated coconut

eggs

butter

sugar

grated lime rind

salt

water

baking powder

lime

plain flour

1 Preheat the oven to 180°C/350°F/ Gas 4. Grease two 23 cm/9 in cake tins and base-line with non-stick baking paper. Sift together the flour, baking powder and salt.

2 Beat the butter in a large bowl, until it is soft and creamy. Beat in the sugar and lime rind until the mixture is pale and fluffy. Beat in the eggs, one at a time.

3 Beat in the sifted dry ingredients in small portions, alternating with the lime juice and water. When the mixture is smooth, gently stir in 40 g/1½ oz/½ cup of the coconut.

4 Divide the mixture between the prepared tins and spread it evenly. Bake for 30–35 minutes or until a skewer inserted in the centre of one of the cakes comes out clean.

5 Cool the cake layers in their tins for 10 minutes. Then turn them out on a wire rack, peel off the lining paper and cool completely.

6 Spread the remaining coconut in a clean dry cake tin. Bake until golden brown, stirring occasionally. Allow to cool completely.

7 Put one of the cake layers, base up, on a serving plate. Spread a layer of frosting evenly over the cake. Set the second layer on top. Spread the remaining frosting all over the top and around the sides of the cake.

8 Scatter the toasted coconut over the top of the cake and allow to set before serving.

Fresh Fruit Genoese

Cakes don't have to be elaborate to taste superb: light sponge, fresh fruit and cream are an unbeatable combination.

Serves 8–10

INGREDIENTS
175 g/6 oz/1½ cups plain flour
pinch of salt
4 eggs
115 g/4 oz/½ cup caster sugar
90 ml/6 tbsp orange-flavoured
    liqueur

FOR THE FILLING AND TOPPING
600 ml/1 pint/2½ cups double cream
60 ml/4 tbsp vanilla sugar
450 g/1 lb fresh soft fruit, such as
    raspberries, blueberries or
    cherries
150 g/5 oz/1¼ cups shelled pistachio
    nuts, finely chopped
60 ml/4 tbsp apricot jam, warmed
    and sieved, to glaze

plain flour

double cream

apricot jam

pistachio nuts

eggs

vanilla sugar   *caster sugar*

orange-flavoured liqueur

fresh soft fruit

1 Preheat the oven to 180°C/350°F/ Gas 4. Grease and base-line a 20 cm/8 in round springform cake tin. Sift the flour and salt together three times.

2 Place the eggs and sugar in a mixing bowl and beat with an electric mixer for about 10 minutes or until thick and pale. Sift the flour mixture over, then fold in very gently. Transfer the cake mixture to the prepared tin. Bake for 30–35 minutes or until a skewer inserted into the cake comes out clean. Leave the cake in the tin for 5 minutes, then turn out on to a wire rack, peel off the lining paper and leave to cool completely. Cut the cake horizontally into two layers, and place the bottom layer on a serving plate. Sprinkle the orange-flavoured liqueur over both layers.

3 Place the double cream and vanilla sugar in a mixing bowl and beat with an electric mixer until it holds peaks.

4 Spread two-thirds of the cream mixture over the bottom layer of the cake and top with half the fruit. Place the second cake layer on top and spread the remaining cream over the top and sides. Lightly press the chopped nuts around the sides. Arrange the remaining fresh fruit on top and brush over the apricot jam to glaze the fruit lightly.

COOK'S TIP
To save time and money, use shop-bought chopped mixed nuts to coat the sides of the gâteau instead of pistachios.

INDEX